DATE DUE

JUN 1 8 2010			
			IY 1 2 2009

Demco, Inc. 38-293

SUNY series, Teacher Preparation and Development
Alan R. Tom, editor

Innovations in Teacher Education

A Social Constructivist Approach

Clive Beck and Clare Kosnik

State University
of New York
Press

Published by
State University of New York Press, Albany

© 2006 State University of New York

For information, address State University of New York Press,
194 Washington Avenue, Suite 305, Albany, NY 12210-2384

Production by Susan Geraghty
Marketing by Anne M. Valentine

Library of Congress Cataloging-in-Publication Data

Beck, Clive.
    Innovations in teacher education : a social constructivist approach /
Clive Beck and Clare Kosnik.
        p. cm. — (SUNY series in teacher preparation and development)
    Includes bibliographical references and index.
    ISBN 0-7914-6717-1 (hardcover : alk. paper) — ISBN 0-7914-6718-X
(pbk. : alk. paper)
    1. Student teachers. 2. Teachers—Training of. 3. Constructivism
(Education) 4. Educational innovations. I. Kosnik, Clare Madott. II.
Title. III. Series.

LB2157.A3B395 2006
370'.71'1—dc22

                                                                        2005014019

ISBN-13: 978-0-7914-6717-6 (hardcover : alk. paper)
ISBN-13: 978-0-7914-6718-3 (pbk. : alk. paper)

                        10 9 8 7 6 5 4 3 2 1

To our colleagues everywhere
in teacher education practice and research

CONTENTS

ACKNOWLEDGMENTS

Developing this book has been an enjoyable collaborative venture, with assistance coming from many groups and individuals. We wish to thank the administrations and preservice faculty at Bank Street College, Edith Cowan University, Mills College, New York University, Stanford University, the University of Sydney, and Teachers College, Columbia University. We were always warmly received on our site-visits and this aspect of the project was a wonderful experience. We are especially grateful, of course, to the faculty we interviewed. They were frank in their responses and generous with their time both during the visits and in reading and correcting the transcripts afterward. Moreover, it was their vision, hard work, and commitment to innovation that gave rise to the examples of best practice on which much of the book is based. At OISE, University of Toronto over the years we have also received outstanding support in our program development and research activities from cohort coordinators, faculty, student teachers, and general administration. At State University of New York Press, Priscilla Ross and Lisa Chesnel have provided strong encouragement and helpful guidance from the beginning. Finally, we wish to extend sincere thanks to Alan Tom, series editor, who has given us invaluable advice and direction based on his extensive experience and scholarship in the field of teacher education. So many of the issues raised and ideas developed here have their origins in what we have learned from him.

INTRODUCTION

Constructivist teaching and teacher education has clearly arrived.
Discussions of these topics dominate scholarly and practitioner journals
in most subject areas.

—Virginia Richardson, *Constructivist Teacher
Education, Building a World of New Understandings*

Preservice teacher education today is a site of contrasting trends. On the one hand, there are promising developments: theory–practice links, cohort groupings, teaching for understanding, reflective practice, school–university partnerships, and self-study research. On the other hand, however, we see cuts in funding, pressure to teach less theory, inadequate alternative certification, stifling accreditation rules, superficial exit tests, and evaluation of programs largely in quantitative terms. There are calls both to expand teacher education and to curtail it. As a result, teacher educators are experiencing both hope and despair.

Faced with these conflicts and pressures, what are we to do? Should we opt for compromise, making concessions to the conservative, transmission-oriented forces? Should we settle for somewhat shorter, simpler, and cheaper programs? In our view, there is no alternative but to continue in the direction of innovation and enhancement of programs. In the case of schooling, it is increasingly clear that the move back to transmission is not resulting in significant gains even in standardized test results, let alone depth of understanding and general student growth (Berliner & Biddle, 1995; Meier, 2000). At the same time, evidence exists that the progressive alternative can be very effective (Darling-Hammond, 1997), and much contemporary educational theory indicates why this is so. Why should we, then, implement in teacher preparation an approach that does not work at the school level? Rather, we need to make a clearer and stronger case for the alternative approach and devise more effective ways to implement it.

But what exactly is this progressive alternative? Our preference is to call it "social constructivism," hence the subtitle of our book. This situates it in the tradition of Dewey, Piaget, and Vygotsky, but at the same time links it to fruitful new strands in sociocultural thought. The term social constructivism is used increasingly today to refer to progressive reforms in education. Virginia

Richardson (1997), a key figure in the field of teaching and teacher education, writes: "Constructivist teaching and teacher education has clearly arrived. Discussions of these topics dominate scholarly and practitioner journals in most subject areas" (p. 3). She describes constructivism as the position that "individuals create their own understandings, based upon the interaction of what they already know and believe, and the phenomena or ideas with which they come in contact" (p. 3). Although originally somewhat individualistic in orientation, constructivism has recently taken on a social emphasis: social factors are seen as crucial "in both the construction and appropriation of knowledge" (p. 7). It is this latter version of constructivism that we wish to propose for utilization in preservice education.

At the school level, social constructivism implies a form of learning in which students are fully engaged, find the process meaningful, and relate ideas to the real world to a considerable extent. Only in this way can they participate in constructing their knowledge and acquire the habits that make them lifelong learners. The teacher fosters a culture in the classroom that supports critical and productive inquiry. There is a strong sense of community and much collaborative learning. The learning experience is holistic: in addition to the social aspect, emotional, aesthetic, bodily, and other forms of expression are involved. This not only allows for broad personal development, but ensures the depth of understanding and experience needed for knowledge construction.

At the preservice level, social constructivism involves a similar kind of culture and experience: meaningful, critical, social, holistic. This is necessary so student teachers can see firsthand what the approach means, learn "how to do it," and grow intellectually and personally in ways necessary for social constructivist teaching. We believe that a small cohort program with its own faculty team is the arrangement usually most conducive to these kinds of outcomes. The case for smallness has been made well by a number of writers on schooling (Meier, 1995; Wasley, 1994; Wood, 1992, 1998), and the same basic arguments can be applied to preservice education. Such conditions facilitate the kind of program integration, close teacher–student relationship, and community experience needed to achieve social constructivist goals. Most of the programs discussed in this book have a small cohort and their own faculty team.

Part of the basis for this book is our own experience in the "Mid-Town" cohort program at OISE, University of Toronto. One of the authors helped establish Mid-Town (then called by a different name) in the late 1980s, and the other author has worked in the program since 1995. Many of the examples in chapters 1, 3, 4, 6, and 7 are drawn from the Mid-Town experience and from the extensive research we have conducted on the program. In this era of "narrative inquiry" and "self-study research" we do not apologize for the focus on our own program, and in fact we think readers will appreciate the detailed account we are able to give of a cohort approach because of our personal involvement.

At the same time, however, we have gone to considerable lengths to provide examples of innovations from other programs as well. Using funds from a small-scale Social Sciences and Humanities Research Council of Canada (SSHRC) project on "Effective Program Structures," we studied seven programs in the United States and Australia. We selected them both because of their cohort structure and because we regarded them as exemplary innovative programs with a social constructivist approach. The U.S. programs are at Bank Street College of Education, Mills College, New York University, Stanford University, and Teachers College, Columbia University; the Australian programs are at Edith Cowan University and the University of Sydney. We are very grateful to SSHRC for funding this research and to the 28 faculty in the various programs for their generous participation. Originally we asked only for anonymous use of information and quotations; however, when they had seen the finished manuscript, all the interviewees graciously consented to have their institutions identified and their real names used. We feel this adds considerable concreteness and human interest to the book.

As indicated, our discussion in this book is to a significant extent research-based. However, the research on Mid-Town was more systematic than that on the other programs. In the latter case, our only data source—apart from published information on the programs—was the faculty interviews (these were usually audiotaped and transcribed; in two instances they were conducted by telephone and email). With the limited funds available, we were not able to interview student teachers or conduct class visits. The research methodology throughout was mainly qualitative. We describe and justify our methodology in chapter 7 in the context of discussing the importance of doing research on one's own preservice program.

We see the main audience for the book as preservice educators and school of education administrators interested in considering ways to enhance their preservice programming. We believe the book contributes significantly to the theory of teacher education; however, the examples and quotations do double duty, both clarifying the theory and providing concrete suggestions on how to establish and maintain the type of social constructivist program we are recommending. We trust that even preservice educators who do not accept the whole model may find parts of it of practical value. Beyond this readership, we hope that faculty and graduate students doing research, writing, and teaching on preservice education may also find the book useful.

Chapter 1 sets out the conceptual framework for the book, focusing primarily on the nature of social constructivism. However, already in this chapter we offer extensive examples of innovations in preservice education that illustrate what we mean by social constructivism. Chapters 2, 3, and 4 are concerned respectively with the themes of integration, inquiry, and community in social constructivist preservice education. These chapters contain the great bulk of the examples from the seven programs we studied in the United States and Australia.

In each of these chapters we highlight just three of the programs; we felt it would be easier for readers to follow the discussion if we did not refer to all the programs in every chapter. We wish to emphasize, however, that all the programs studied embody integration, inquiry, and community to a high degree.

The remaining chapters are shorter, and we draw examples from many programs referred to in the research literature rather than just the ones we studied (in chapters 6 and 7 a great deal of material from our Mid-Town program is included). Chapter 5, which is on equity and inclusion in preservice education, makes the argument that inclusion is not just an "add-on," but rather social constructivism *entails* an inclusive approach, given its emphasis on critical inquiry, respect for the other, and genuine community. In chapter 6, the case is made for reaching out beyond our own cohort program to the school of education and university as a whole, with a view to extending our influence and gaining greater support. This is essential given the challenges that often face preservice programs, such as excessive workload, inadequate resources, and lack of respect and reward for preservice faculty. We give detailed suggestions on how such challenges may be addressed. In chapter 7, as noted, we discuss the importance of doing research on our own preservice program, as well as broader research that links back to our own program. Conducting such research not only strengthens our program but also helps increase our influence and support within the larger institution.

The terminology employed in the book is generalized to take account of the fact that we are referring to different programs in different countries and intending our discussion to be helpful to yet other programs in other countries. We follow the common practice of using the term "SCDE" to refer generally to schools, colleges, departments, and faculties of education. The term "university," here, covers both colleges and universities. We use "mentor teachers" in relation to teachers variously called "cooperating," "associate," and "host teachers." The term "practicum" is used whether there is just one practicum placement or several, and covers both formal and informal field experiences. We use the term "student teacher" or "student" most of the time rather than "teacher candidate" or "preservice teacher," because we feel the term "candidate" is a little too bureaucratic in tone and because calling preservice students "teachers," while suitably respectful, can be confusing and in fact is seldom done in practice. (We do not feel strongly about this point, however, and are still looking for a better term.) The expression "preservice education" here covers a wide range of types of programs, including ones in which student teachers have a considerable amount of autonomous teaching experience, but are still pursuing an initial teacher qualification. Finally, we use the term "postbaccalaureate" rather than "graduate" to refer to programs in which students already have a university degree, because some such programs just lead to a diploma in education (as at Edith Cowan) or a further bachelor's degree (as in our own B.Ed.) and not to a master's degree.

In conclusion, we wish to emphasize that we are not offering here a blueprint for preservice education but rather a set of ideas, principles, and sample structures and practices. We believe the specific examples we provide are useful because they show what can be done, despite the challenges, and suggest strategies that may be useful elsewhere. However, our main concern is to propose certain goals and standards, in a sense, for preservice education, and continue a conversation about directions for our field. In accordance with social constructivist theory, readers must treat these suggestions as grist for the mill and arrive at approaches and strategies that fit their own beliefs, values, and circumstances. Preservice education is so demanding that, in order to continue in it, we must have a strong sense of ownership and be personally convinced of the worthwhileness of what we are doing.

CHAPTER 1

Toward Social Constructivism in Preservice Education

[E]ducation is not an affair of "telling" and being told, but an active and constructive process.
> —John Dewey, *Democracy and Education*

As stated in the introduction, we believe social constructivism can provide crucial direction for preservice education and we see evidence of it in the strong, innovative programs described in this book. But what exactly is meant by this term? As Richardson (1997) notes, constructivist teaching is not "a monolithic, agreed-upon concept" (p. 3). It is often barely understood, or actually misunderstood. For example, some identify it just as an activity approach, overlooking its role in empowering learners and critiquing prevailing ideas and social practices. Others understand it as unstructured "discovery learning," where anything goes. Still others interpret it as a highly subjective and individualistic process that neglects experience of the world and collaboration with others. Misunderstandings of these kinds give constructivism a bad name and create obstacles to gaining support and resources for constructivist teaching and teacher education; they also make implementation of the approach difficult even under ideal conditions.

In this chapter, through discussion and examples, we will attempt to clarify the nature of social constructivism, and we will continue to illustrate it throughout the book, especially with reference to preservice programming. In exploring social constructivism, we will draw on past interpretations of constructivism, notably, those of Dewey, Piaget, and Vygotsky, and also bring insights from more recent writers on sociocultural theory, such as Foucault, Derrida, and Rorty. By its own tenets, social constructivism is constantly changing and open to a variety of interpretations. We will present here our own understanding of the approach; and, in constructivist spirit, we invite readers to develop *their* interpretation, in part in response to ours.

However, we will argue strongly for our interpretation, because we believe much is at stake and some ways of conducting teacher education are better than others. On our understanding, social constructivism is an approach that encourages all members of a learning community to present their ideas strongly, while remaining open to the ideas of others. It is a passionate approach, involving the whole person: thought, emotion, and action. It is not a relativistic outlook, where just any position will do. Like Nuthall (2002), we think teacher input has a major role within a social constructivist framework. However, we also stress that students, too, must have a major role, with greater opportunity than they commonly have to give input, discuss, and reflect in class. Just how much weight to give to individual, teacher, and peer input respectively must be the subject of ongoing study and debate.

Social constructivism is not just an interesting theoretical idea; it can help significantly with challenges and tensions we face in teacher education today. For example, preservice educators are familiar with the problem of the gap between the university classroom and the school. Fostering a progressive approach among student teachers despite the cover-and-test culture in schools today presents a huge challenge. There is also the crisis of a high attrition rate among teachers. The gulf between academic knowledge and popular culture is a further problem. We believe a social constructivist approach to preservice education has potential to assist with these pressing difficulties, as well as others. Our main concern in this book is to consider how this might be done.

A central reason for fostering social constructivism in preservice education is to help make teaching a more attractive and respected profession. That will not happen if we return to a transmission approach. We are constantly impressed with the very high caliber of people who decide to become teachers. They have strong academic backgrounds, are vibrant and outgoing, and have a passion for interacting with students and helping them academically and in other ways. At the same time, schooling is under siege, conditions for teachers are often frustrating and demeaning, and the level of burnout is high. While improving working conditions and increasing resources for teachers must be priorities, we believe high-quality preservice education is also essential to enhance the experience of teachers and their students.

We are appalled when we see universities siphoning off funds earned by teacher education to use for other purposes, and when we hear of proposals to reduce preservice programs to 3 or 4 months. Granted, we teacher educators have not always done the best job possible. But teacher education is so vital in the whole education enterprise that we should devote more rather than less time, resources, and effort to it. To enhance teacher education significantly, however, we need a better sense of direction. As Sosniak (1999) says, "we need to consider redeveloping a curriculum for teacher education more consistent with what we value" (p. 200). We believe that a more fully developed and implemented social constructivism can take us toward what we value for ourselves, our young people, and society as a whole.

But despite the promise, there is a serious question whether a social constructivist approach is generally feasible in preservice education. As teacher educators face larger classes, heavier teaching loads, higher research and publishing expectations, low teacher morale in schools, and widespread government pressure toward transmission education, how can we implement social constructivism? Student teachers themselves often question the viability of such an approach, under current conditions.

It seems to us the approach is feasible, given that it is already being practiced in many places. But we would agree that if it is to be implemented more widely and sustained over time, greater support is needed from schools of education, the university as a whole, and beyond. The exploration of social constructivism that follows is intended to provide a firmer basis both for gaining such support and for implementing the approach.

OVERVIEW OF SOCIAL CONSTRUCTIVISM

Social constructivism is a very complex approach; throughout the book we will continue to attempt to define and illustrate it. In this chapter, we will introduce the paradigm. In the first section we will outline what we regard as its key principles. As we give our interpretation of each principle, we will cite relevant authors and discuss briefly the implications of the principle for preservice education, presenting one or two examples from our own program at OISE/University of Toronto. In the second section of the chapter we will further clarify the nature of the approach by describing recent social constructivist trends in teacher education.

Knowledge is constructed by learners. All constructivists, whatever their distinctive emphasis, agree that learners construct their knowledge. Hence the term constructivism. As Dewey (1916) said, "education is not an affair of 'telling' and being told, but an active and constructive process" (p. 46). Even when we use other people's ideas, we assess and modify them rather than just absorbing them in a preset form.

Constructing our own knowledge is necessary in part because that is how the mind works. We cannot grasp new ideas without linking them to existing concepts. According to Dewey (1916), "no thought, no idea, can possibly be conveyed as an idea from one person to another." Learners must interpret new ideas in the context of their present interests and understandings if they are to have thoughts at all (p. 188). For example, if we are considering for the first time the idea that teacher–student dialogue is important for learning, we need our previous concepts of "teacher" and "student" as a basis for pondering this insight. At a later stage we may modify these concepts to make them consistent with the new insight, but this again will be a gradual process, building on earlier concepts.

Another reason why we must construct our own knowledge is to ensure that it is useful. From a constructivist viewpoint, the primary purpose of knowledge is to help humans function in the world, not to describe universal reality (Dewey, 1929/1960; Rorty, 1979). According to Vadeboncoeur (1997), Piaget maintained that "[l]earners construct ways to make sense of experiences, and will continue to use those constructions as long as they work" (p. 23). Ideas that "work" are ones that are suited to our needs and circumstances and so take us in appropriate directions. For example, our concept of good literature should lead us to works we find interesting and enjoyable and can discuss with our friends. More sophisticated ideas about literature may eventually have a valuable impact on our lives, but at a particular stage they may be alienating and even discourage us from reading.

The fact that we construct our knowledge does not mean it is just an individual, subjective matter, without external reference. On the contrary, our knowledge is heavily influenced by experience of life and the world (Foucault, 1998; Phillips, 1995) and by dialogue with others (Dewey, 1938; Piaget, 1932). Even direct instruction, commonly associated with transmission pedagogy, can play an important role in constructivist learning (Brophy, 2002). But while these external influences are essential, we must adapt ideas to a considerable extent if they are to have meaning and value in our lives.

A key implication of the constructivist paradigm for teacher education is that student teachers should have time and encouragement to reflect on what they are learning. Because of the short duration of preservice programs there is a tendency to think we must "give them the theory" while we have the chance, leaving them to work out the implications as they teach. This is an unfortunate approach, however, not only because it models transmission pedagogy but because it gives the students inadequate opportunity to assess and adapt theory (Fosnot, 1989; Tom, 1997; Wideen & Lemma, 1999). In our own preservice program, which is just 9 months long, we build in as much time as possible for personal reflection, discussion of implications, and expression of alternative views. Sometimes students complain that there is too much reflection and discussion. They would like us just to tell them what to teach at each grade level and which activities to use, believing this would be more efficient and would prepare them better. But we feel that one of our main tasks in the program is to encourage them to move away from this passive view of learning.

With encouragement and support, our students begin to develop a teaching style that fits their distinctive needs and talents. For example, those who are especially energized by interacting with pupils and helping them in a variety of ways make this a major emphasis in their teaching, while those who gain much satisfaction from intellectual engagement and seeing students grasp key ideas place this at the center of their pedagogy. Both types of goals are important, of course, but differences in emphasis are necessary if these new teachers are to find their work fulfilling and give maximum help to their students.

A more specific example of individual construction of pedagogy is seen in our students' approach to technology in education. Those who have had many positive experiences with technology tend to make it central to their view of education, seeing topics, strategies, and even goals through this lens. By contrast, those who are uncomfortable with technology typically think of teaching in terms of discussion, reading, art activities, and so forth, with technology a discrete skill used on particular occasions. Although it is important for student teachers to integrate technology as much as possible, allowing differences of degree facilitates optimal teacher development and performance.

Knowledge is experience-based. A further reason why learners should construct knowledge is to utilize their rich experience. The knowledge developed by academics is usually too abstract, as it stands, to be useful in everyday situations. As Dewey (1938) said:

> [A]ll principles by themselves are abstract. They become concrete only in the consequences which result from their application. . . . [E]verything depends upon the interpretation given them as they are put into practice in the school and the home. (p. 20)

Learners must bring their detailed knowledge to bear in interpreting general principles (Schön, 1983).

Ordinary learners (as distinct from experts) not only reinterpret existing concepts and principles, they frequently develop new ones based on their experience of the world. Although they use different tools and language from experts, they often investigate the same phenomena and make a substantial contribution to knowledge (Rorty, 1989). For example, ordinary people develop complex principles and strategies for relating to fellow family members, even though this is also the domain of moral philosophers, family psychologists, and so on. They may in fact devise major new approaches to family life, resulting in changes in the conception of the family. Such changes are not mere addenda to expert theory; rather, they involve a basic recentering of thought (Derrida, 1972/1982). In discussing the field of education, Carr (1995) points to "the extensive theoretical powers that educational practitioners already possess" and the fact that basic pedagogical theory is often "generated out of the experience of practitioners" (pp. 34–35).

This view of the close connection between knowledge and experience is relevant to teacher education. In theory classes in our preservice program we rely heavily on the experience of student teachers. Although we too have past and current experience of schooling, the sheer range of the students' experiential background offers a rich resource. A topic raised recently in a School and Society class concerned how to teach small groups of students withdrawn from regular class for special literacy help. Drawing on their experiences in the first practicum, the student teachers provided many examples of the varied attitudes and ability levels of these students, conflicting directives from inside and outside the school about what to do with them, and effective strategies for helping each type of student. These examples shed light on the complexity of the issues and resulted in a highly nuanced approach to the topic.

The student teachers sometimes take a position that leads to a major restructuring of our ideas about teaching and learning. For example, one year we decided to have an early class on the "stages of teacher development" from "novice" through "competent" to "expert" level. We thought it would give students a sense of direction in their growth as teachers and pride in the high attainments of their profession. However, almost the whole cohort objected vociferously to this stage model. They saw it as stereotyping, demeaning for them, and likely to stifle innovative practice in their teaching placements. Their reaction led us to abandon this way of talking and search for a more appropriate model of differences between new and experienced teachers.

Learning is social. The ideas discussed so far apply to constructivism in general. The principle that learning is social, on the other hand, relates especially to *social* constructivism. Although Piaget stressed social factors (e.g., Piaget, 1932), Vygotsky and later writers developed this perspective further and in new ways. Like Piaget, they noted the importance of dialogue with others in knowledge construction. Vygotsky in particular spoke of the importance of teacher–student dialogue, and the need for teachers to stimulate learning within a "zone" consistent with each student's current level of development (Vygotsky, 1978). Adding to Piaget, however, social constructivists have explored the direct impact of language and culture on learners, an impact that often occurs without dialogue and beyond learners' conscious control (Barthes, 1970/1982; Foucault, 1998; Vygotsky, 1978).

Many social constructivists are concerned mainly with the effects of the larger society on knowledge formation; others focus especially on the role of "learning communities" created within educational institutions. The impact of the larger society is often negative and accidental. By contrast, a well-developed class community can have a positive influence in a broadly anticipated direction (Brophy, 2002; Dewey, 1916). For example, such a community can give strong social and emotional support, thus enabling learners to take risks and develop ownership of their learning. It can also provide opportunities for democratic dialogue during which the ideas presented by teachers are modified (Benhabib, 1990). Along these lines, Wells (1994) describes Vygotsky's social constructivism in terms of a two-way process:

> As the learner appropriates the knowledge and procedures encountered in interaction with others, he or she transforms them, constructing his or her own personal version. But in the process, he or she is also transformed. . . . (p. 8)

The knowledge teachers possess is important for fruitful dialogue (Nuthall, 2002), but the knowledge students bring to the classroom is also essential.

Of course, all the social learning that takes place in educational institutions is by no means positive. Such institutions often mirror problematic features of the larger society and add others of their own (Bourdieu, 1977; Lyotard, 1984). Dewey (1916) spoke of the need for the school to be a "purified" environment, with a higher level of sociability, personal security, and stimulus for growth than is commonly experienced. Social constructivists advocate forming learning communities that are not only nurturing and supportive but also engage in constant critique of social and educational institutions.

We have observed the positive impact of a learning community in our preservice program (Beck & Kosnik, 2001). Because the student teachers feel secure in the community, they make very frank comments to faculty about such matters as the content and methodology of our courses, the texts we use, our views on particular topics, the timing of assignments, and evaluation methods for practice teaching. They also share with us and their peers their early doubts about being a teacher arising from the rigors of practice teaching and the less than ideal conditions in schools, and specific difficulties they are experiencing in teaching, notably with classroom management. These types of sharing give rise to dialogue that is instructive for both students and faculty.

All aspects of a person are connected. On a social constructivist view, knowledge is dependent not only on social interaction, as discussed previously, but on all other aspects of the person: attitudes, emotions, values, and actions. The paradigm is strongly *holistic*. Dewey argued continually against dualisms in thought and life, in particular the "opposition of flesh and spirit" (Dewey, 1934/1980, p. 20). Similarly, Barthes (1977), Foucault (1998), and Derrida (1967/1978) have stressed connections between knowledge, pleasure, ethics, aesthetics, the body, and human action. In our view, constructivists in education have sometimes given a disproportionate emphasis to knowledge formation within *disciplines*. While the discipline context is very important, knowledge ultimately has meaning within a set of values (Sternberg, 2003) or indeed a way of life. Students in school need extensive opportunity and support to develop their whole way of life and bring this to bear systematically on their academic learning.

One aspect of this holistic perspective is recognition of the connection between knowledge and popular culture. Schooling is often seen as overcoming the negative influence of popular culture, such as TV, movies, comic books, popular music, and fashion. However, on a social constructivist view both academic knowledge and popular culture can have either a negative or positive impact. Both can seduce or bring insight, indoctrinate or enhance life. Social constructivists minimize the contrast between the academic and popular domains (Barthes, 1970/1982; Derrida, 1967/1978; Rorty, 1989). For education, this means supporting expression and discussion of popular culture in the classroom and critiquing academic knowledge in light of popular culture, as well as the converse.

In our preservice program we encourage student teachers to express many aspects of themselves—to "be themselves"—within the preservice program. For example, students who are parents bring that part of their life to the community, talking about their situation and how it affects their personal and professional experience. Similarly, students who are athletes or musicians tell us about their activities in these areas, and we often attend their competitions and performances. We find this has a positive impact not only on these individuals but also on the rest of the cohort, helping them see the connection between teaching and family life, the body, aesthetic life, and so on. It helps humanize their approach to teaching.

We also encourage our student teachers to be up-front about their involvement with popular culture: the internet, video games, rock music, popular dance, and so on. From the beginning, the getting-to-know-you activities explore such interests and this continues at the retreat, on the cohort internet conference, and at social events. We do not want them to see teaching or the preservice program as just concerned with the academic or "serious" side of life. In the celebratory activities at the end of the year, these popular elements are apparent as the graduating teachers present humorous and revealing skits and video clips about their experience in the program.

Learning communities should be inclusive and equitable. Several of the principles noted so far, such as the need to tailor knowledge to people's lives and the social nature of learning, point toward inclusiveness and equity in learning. Dewey and Piaget stressed inclusion within the learning community and helping children develop a sense of dignity and their own ideas and way of life. Later theorists have explored these themes more fully, advocating a strongly critical perspective. Barthes (1970/1982), Bourdieu (1977), Foucault (1997), and Lyotard (1984) describe how established culture and knowledge often oppress non-mainstream groups; they call for systematic analysis and criticism to reduce these effects. Derrida (1990) emphasizes the responsibility of institutions to acknowledge the difference of "the other" and work to support people in constructing reality from their distinctive point of view. Rorty (1985) proposes the formation of inclusive communal groups with a strong sense of solidarity.

In our preservice program we establish and model an inclusive community, and we have found that student teachers respond well to such an approach (Beck & Kosnik, 2001). We have observed a remarkable level of caring toward all members of the cohort community, including those of different gender, race, ethnicity, class, sexual orientation, and physical ability. Within a close community, student teachers get to know one another and develop a "we" outlook that generally reduces barriers existing in the larger society. Moreover, they quickly see the relevance of this experience for their own teaching, coming to regard building inclusive communities as one of the most important aspects of their role. While they will continue to encounter prejudice and discrimination of various kinds in "the real world," we believe this experience of a community that is relatively inclusive and is trying to move further in that direction will be of help to them both personally and professionally. It will be a memorable experience of a different approach to interpersonal relationships and community life that has application within education and beyond.

Every year in our program we have at least one or two students who comment that they could not have survived the preservice experience without the acceptance and support of their peers and the faculty team. These have included, for example, women with young children, unmarried mothers, students in severe financial difficulties, and students with a history of abuse in their upbringing. While it might be argued that some of these people will have difficulty managing in the even tougher early years of teaching, in our experience they often blossom and become strong in the program and go on to be very successful teachers. Furthermore, they bring significantly different perspectives to the cohort, as they will as teachers after graduation. We believe it is crucially important to encourage such people to enter preservice education and support them strongly while they are there. A social constructivist program is well suited to achieving these goals.

SOCIAL CONSTRUCTIVIST TRENDS IN PRESERVICE EDUCATION

As mentioned earlier, innovations have already occurred in a social constructivist direction in preservice education, especially in the past couple of decades (Richardson, 1997); precedents exist from which one can learn in pursuing this line of thought and practice. In later chapters we will give detailed examples of programs that have developed such an approach. Here we present just an outline of recent trends in preservice education to illustrate further the general concept of social constructivism. We begin the discussion of each trend by noting the particular features of social constructivism it embodies.

A life history approach to teaching. Lortie (1975) noted how new teachers frequently teach the way they were taught. Increasingly in preservice programs the previous life experiences of student teachers, including their prior schooling, are being treated as relevant. Through a variety of activities students reflect on their experiences of life and learning and relate them to their views on education. This approach is constructivist in several ways. It acknowledges that new ideas must be based in part on old ones, and hence learning to teach is a gradual process rather than a sudden initiation. It recognizes that knowledge must make sense in terms of a person's whole way of life: one cannot separate the professional from the personal, the academic from the everyday. And it accepts the contribution of one's rich prior experience to knowing how to teach.

Explicitly stating that her preservice teaching is grounded in Vygotsky's thought, Samaras (1998) describes how students in her program "examine their past schooling experiences and beliefs about teaching, and negotiate and reconstruct meanings about teaching after embodying the voices of others" (p. 64). She presents as an illustration her "education-related life history" assignment:

> This assignment asks students to write about the following: how they came to the decision to be a teacher, their notions and doubts about teaching, important people and critical incidents that influenced their decision to teach, and implications of their school experiences for their notions of teaching. I open the class discussion by talking about my early schooling. . . . I ask students to share the highlights of their stories. (p. 65).

Knowles, Cole, and Presswood (1994) stress the extent to which student teachers already have relevant knowledge when they enter the preservice program. They go so far as to say that student teachers "are themselves teacher educators," whose experiences should be "the starting points for reflection, discussion, and inquiry" (p. viii). Preservice programs should reveal inquiry into "self, contexts, and relationships" as an essential and lifelong aspect of professional development: among other things, such inquiry fosters personal and professional empowerment (p. viii). One of the forms of autobiographical writing the authors advocate is "personal history accounts":

> Each of us possesses personal histories that are rich and intensely interesting. By personal or life history accounts we mean stories of your experiences of learning in formal and informal settings . . . and the meanings you attribute to those experiences. . . . Personal history accounts are not intended to be exclusively chronological records of events but, rather, to be examinations of your efforts to become a teacher within the context of your educational life. . . . Some potentially useful topics to explore and to start you writing include: your decision to become a teacher, teachers' work, visions of teachers and teaching, outstanding teachers and their influence on you, metaphors for teaching and working with students in classrooms. . . . (pp. 22–23, 29)

Schoonmaker (2002), in her significantly titled book *"Growing Up" Teaching: From Personal Knowledge to Professional Practice*, maintains that learning to teach "should be recognized as a process of continuous reconstruction of experience" (p. x), and that "all learning—including that about theory and its relation to curricular practice and classroom/social control—passes through the individual's mental and emotional filters (pp. 57–58). She emphasizes, however, that student teachers bring both positive and problematic understandings of schooling from their earlier experiences. For example, one student whom she studied in depth came with a sense that schooling should be "fun and rewarding" and "fair" to students, but also with a rather traditional conception of appropriate teaching content and activities. She advocates respecting both types of views in a preservice program. The positive ones—for example, that learning should be fun—need to be qualified and deepened, and the problematic ones should similarly be used as starting points for deconstruction and reconstruction.

School-based research by student teachers. In addition to reflection on past life experiences and developments, many preservice programs have student teachers conduct research in schools and classrooms. This component is constructivist in that it implies that teachers should build their own theory and practice of teaching based on their experiences and observations, rather than just applying the findings and principles of university-based researchers. It also underscores an inquiry approach to teaching, since it sees a teacher's pedagogy continuing to evolve over the years through constant reassessment. Further, such an approach reflects the nonauthoritarian outlook of constructivism since the research typically involves listening to students and taking account of their views.

Action research is one of the main forms of research incorporated into preservice programs. Ross (1987) has been a pioneer in this development. She points out that, because campus courses are often rather separate from the practicum, practice teaching can reinforce a transmission approach to teaching:

> While [student teachers'] attitudes may become more progressive as they take coursework in education . . . their experiences in public schools during their internships encourage them to focus on learning "what works" with little consideration of broader educational objectives and principles. . . . By the time most students complete their final field experiences they have become "passive technicians who merely learn to execute pre-packaged instructional programs" (Goodman, 1986, p. 112). (Ross, 1987, p. 131)

By contrast, having action research as a component in the program can help student teachers "view teaching as integrally related to research and as a process that involves inquiry and experimentation" (p. 147).

Zeichner (1990) reports that many recent innovations in preservice education are designed to prepare "teachers who are researchers of their practice" (p. 115). These innovations vary in precise form, but they all use the practicum "as a site for furthering teaching as a form of research and experimentation" (p. 115). Liston and Zeichner (1991) describe the inquiry component of the elementary teacher education program at the University of Wisconsin–Madison, which was initiated to try to overcome the preoccupation of student teachers with "mastery of teaching skills within the classroom" to the neglect of the goals those skills are meant to serve (p. 166). This inquiry component includes three different kinds of activities: action research, ethnographic studies, and curriculum analysis. The authors outline the action research element as follows:

Student teachers spend a portion of their weekly seminar time discussing and reacting to one another's developing projects, and they prepare written accounts of the evolution of their projects at the end of the semester. The university supervisor and sometimes the cooperating teacher, as well, seek to facilitate students' inquiries by reacting to them along the way. . . . The university supervisor frequently structures opportunities both for student teachers to learn about and discuss various research strategies (e.g., collecting data about pupil learning) and for student teachers to support their peers' research efforts. Some of the student projects have included experimentation with different grouping procedures within the classroom to assess the effects of alternative strategies for maintaining pupil involvement, examinations of a student teacher's behavior toward high- and low-ability groups, and the careful monitoring of efforts to introduce cooperative learning into the classroom. (pp. 170–71)

Apart from action research projects there are other activities and assignments that emphasize a research or inquiry approach to teaching, such as individual child studies, studies of a particular school, and reflection papers based in part on classroom experiences. For example, in the MET program at the University of Hawaii, an assignment called "Portrait of the School" is designed to help preservice students be more than passive observers in their practicum school. Students use qualitative research strategies to explore the complexities of schools and schooling, looking beyond their classroom to the school as a whole (Beck, Freese, & Kosnik, 2004). Samaras (2002) describes another type of project focused on the dilemmas student teachers face in implementing theory and skills learned in their university courses.

[This project] structures the development of preservice teachers' personal decision making and action in dynamic teaching situations. . . . Through inquiry into dilemmas found in practice, preservice teachers discuss actions and strategies that are based on professional knowledge, careful observation, and reflection. They are asked to consider the consequences, both positive and negative, of their actions. They write about their dilemmas, multiple perspectives, and alternative action plans. . . . During the practicum and student teacher seminars, students make meaning of their individual observations through much dialogue with their peers and professors. (p. 23)

Self-study of teacher education practices. Zeichner (1998) observes that research on teacher education is increasingly conducted by teacher educators themselves, a trend that in his view is very positive: "The birth of the self-study in teacher education movement around 1990 has been probably the single most significant development ever in the field of teacher education research" (p. 19). The term self-study in this context has a complex meaning, including personal involvement in research, personal narrative, critical inquiry, respect for experience, and a collaborative approach (Beck, Freese, & Kosnik, 2004).

Although in a sense this trend is not in preservice programs but rather in research on such programs, it indicates that preservice faculty have adopted a social constructivist approach to their own learning about teaching, and this in turn will be reflected in their preservice teaching and programming. As faculty research their practice they gain a fuller understanding of what teacher research means and so are better equipped to help their students move in this direction. Further, their modeling of this approach gives their students concrete examples of how it is done. It also assures the students that such an approach to teaching will be rewarded—and not merely talked about—in the program, thus encouraging them to take an experimental approach in the practicum.

At Queens' University, Russell (2002) conducted self-study research on his role as a "faculty liaison" during the initial 9-week preservice practicum, where he had the dual mandate of supporting student teachers in their placement and enhancing school–university partnerships. He notes that he had a prior assumption that "simply being in the school" would lead to success in the role. However, "[p]ersonal experience and self-study of that experience have taught me how much more complex the matter is" (p. 74). As is the practice in constructivist teaching generally, a major component of his inquiry was observing the students closely and seeking their views; the opinions of school personnel were also solicited.

The study took place over 5 years, from 1997 to 2002. In the program year 1999–2000, for example, Russell made 7 full-day visits to each of the two schools for which he was responsible. There were 13 student teachers in these schools, and he sought their feedback. He commented:

> To help the 13 candidates in 1999–2000 better understand their first action research experience, I explained that I would conduct action research of my own to better understand my contributions to their professional learning. Some showed little interest in providing me with "backtalk" . . . while others were quite willing to do so. (p. 77)

One thing Russell learned that year was that "one size does not fit all"— the differing situations and personal characteristics of student teachers require an individualized approach (pp. 77–78). Another finding was that "most candidates place greatest value on my watching them teach full lessons and providing detailed comments and suggestions" (p. 78). A further theme that emerged from the student interviews was that "[p]ositive reinforcement is as much, if not more, beneficial than negative reinforcement—tell us what we are doing correctly or offer suggestions for improvement" (p. 78). In response to these findings Russell made significant changes to his practice the following year, notably ensuring that wherever possible he observed a full lesson and then discussed it with the student teacher.

In conclusion Russell states that the research made him reconsider his earlier view "that visits to schools to observe preservice candidates are, in and of themselves, valuable to all concerned" (p. 84). More generally, "[t]his self-study of my own efforts to learn the role of faculty liaison over a five-year period has been productive both practically and conceptually." It helped him see that "genuine partnerships may emerge from a base of significant time spent with candidates and experienced teachers, unpacking not only observations of candidates' teaching but also our fundamental premises about teachers' professional learning" (pp. 85–86).

Berry and Loughran (2002) describe self-study research conducted during the development of a new preservice course at Monash University. A central focus of the research, in keeping with their social constructivist approach, was how to build trust in student teachers so they will take risks in class. Establishing trust is usually seen as a gradual process, but they believed it could be achieved from the beginning provided the instructors immediately showed their own willingness to be vulnerable. As they closely observed the impact of their intervention on the students and each other, they became more aware of the complexities of this aspect of teacher education. Yes, a high degree of trust and risk taking can be achieved at an early stage; but "there are still differences between the teacher educator and the student teacher that can inhibit learning through these experiences" (p. 28). Moreover, the vulnerability required of instructors to reach this goal is very challenging for some. As Berry noted in her journal:

> When I heard the students say in response to [Zoe's] teaching "I felt belittled when you asked us to write notes," and "I felt afraid to put my ideas forward when I heard how you responded to' others," it . . . reminded me . . . how vulnerable a position the teacher is in. No matter how much we support the idea of professional critique, it can still be pretty demoralizing to hear what some students are actually thinking and feeling. (p. 25)

This research in the first year of the course led to substantial changes in the second year. For example, as the coordinator of the course Berry began to take more account of the needs and concerns of her fellow instructors, in addition to those of the student teachers.

Cohort groupings and faculty teams. Increasingly today preservice students are being grouped into relatively small cohorts, with a view to enhancing collaboration and community in the program. This shift is due in part to Lortie's (1975) observation that teachers are not adequately "socialized" into the profession, and Goodlad's finding that, typically, there is not "a process through which students planning to teach are socialized together" (Goodlad, 1990b, p. 28). In the 29 universities Goodlad studied, the norm was that "students scarcely knew each other when they came together for the first time in a foundations course. The group assembled was not homogeneous with respect to the goal of teaching, and in no way was it a cohort group, aware of being together in the class of 1992" (Goodlad, 1990a, p. 207).

In the cohort programs emerging over the past two decades, reduced size is achieved either by limiting enrolment or by dividing the students into subgroups (Howey, 1996). A related development is to have the students in a cohort engage in many of their course and field activities together, under the guidance of a team of faculty who work together to achieve an optimal degree of integration both between campus courses and between the campus program and the practicum. This approach is social constructivist most obviously because it emphasizes the social and communal dimension of learning. It is also holistic, helping to integrate different aspects of students' experience, notably the social with the professional and the theoretical with the practical. Further, it provides a solid framework for establishing an inclusive approach to teaching and learning in the preservice program.

A longstanding example of a cohort and faculty team approach is found at the University of Utah, where such programs were begun in the early 1980s (initially at the secondary level, later at the elementary level as well). The Utah initiative "grew out of a perception of the disconnectedness of individual courses and the feeling that there was really no 'program' in any sense of the word" (Arends & Winitzky, 1996, p. 546). Under the arrangement, teacher candidates are organized into cohorts for their final year of pedagogical studies; for three quarters of that year, "candidates take the same classes together, pursue field experiences together in the two or three PDS sites assigned to each cohort, and lend each other professional and moral support" (Winitzky, Stoddart, & O'Keefe, 1992, pp. 11–12).

Each cohort at Utah has a "cohort leader," who is a tenure-track or clinical faculty member; methods faculty rotate in and out of the cohort, but the cohort leader stays with them for the whole year, taking "responsibility for helping students integrate information across methods classes, facilitating clinical assignments, supervising candidates, and helping methods faculty coordinate their courses with each other and with cooperating teachers" (Arends & Winitzky, 1996, pp. 546–47). As a result of adopting the cohort approach it has become possible to experiment with different approaches; in particular, faculty are able to explore the same concepts in both the classroom and the field and keep revisiting these concepts throughout the year (Bullough & Gitlin, 1995, pp. 5–6). According to Arends and Winitzky,

> [The cohorts] have become one of the most positively regarded aspects of the Utah program, highly rated on in-house surveys by teacher candidates and cooperating teachers alike. Candidates report that they appreciate the support system and collegiality that come from the cohort organization. (p. 547)

At Portland State University teacher education has evolved "from a four-year undergraduate program to a fifth-year, graduate teacher preparation program that features thematic cohorts of students" (Peterson, Benson, Driscoll, Narode, Sherman, & Tama, 1995, p. 29). The cohorts are made up of 15 to 30 students who are together for the year-long program.

> [The student teachers] take classes together, are grouped in field placements, experience retreats and team building activities, share a faculty team, and engage in reflection about their work. Each cohort has an identified faculty leader and staff of instructors and supervisors. (p. 30)

Although each cohort has a distinctive thematic focus, there is a common program framework that insures competence in "planning, curriculum, instruction, pupil assessment, classroom management, teacher reflection, and professional development" (p. 30). As a result of the cohort and faculty team structure, students have access to the same faculty throughout the year; key topics can be revisited again and again in different contexts; course theory and classroom practice are integrated; there is considerable flexibility with respect to content, methods, materials, and field placements; and closer collaboration occurs between the program and the partner schools (pp. 30–33). While there was some opposition initially to adopting the cohort approach, it is now viewed very positively by both faculty and school personnel (p. 36).

School-university partnerships. One of the most widely discussed trends in preservice education over the past two decades has been the building of school–university partnerships. This has often meant the establishment of professional development schools (PDSs), with a formal agreement between a university and school to work together in preservice and inservice teacher education, school-based research, and school renewal (Darling-Hammond, 1994). Alternatively, there have been less formal arrangements with similar features: a close working relationship, exchange of staff and ideas, and clustering of a number of student teachers in each school (Goodlad, 1994). The main purpose of having such partnerships is to ensure that student teachers see many examples of good practice during their field experiences and receive the support they need to teach in an experimental, innovative manner. This model is social constructivist in several ways. It stresses a critical inquiry approach to schooling; links theory and practice; and emphasizes caring for "the whole student teacher" in the practicum, often the most stressful aspect of the program.

Drawing on a number of recent studies, Darling-Hammond (1999) describes how preservice programs use PDSs to expose student teachers to state-of-the-art practice and a purposefully structured clinical experience, in a manner comparable to that in teaching hospitals. She reports:

> In the most highly developed sites, programs are jointly planned and taught by university-based and school-based faculty. Cohorts of beginning teachers get a richer, more coherent learning experience when they are organized in

teams to study and practice with these faculty and with one another. Senior teachers report that they deepen their knowledge by serving as mentors, adjunct faculty, co-researchers, and teacher leaders. Thus these schools can help create the rub between theory and practice that teachers need in order to learn. (p. 232)

We see here how the cohort and faculty team structure, described earlier, interacts with the school–university partnership arrangement to produce a set of conditions conducive to social constructivist preservice education.

Fosnot (1996) maintains that, to achieve a constructivist teacher education program, field experiences must take place in settings that are conducive to experimentation and in which curriculum is approached "in an integrated, learner-centered fashion with emphasis on learner investigation, reflection, and discourse" (p. 206). To realize these conditions, she and her colleagues established a small program and formed partnerships with five schools, providing intensive inservice experiences for cooperating teachers from these schools. An unusual feature of their approach was that cooperating teachers and student teachers took courses together. For example, the program began with a 3-week summer institute attended by the cohort of 30 students and 15 teachers from the partnership sites.

This institute, Teaching and Learning I, was team-taught by education and liberal arts faculty. In this institute, participants were involved in constructivist-based learning experiences (on the adult level) in order to provide them with shared opportunities to analyze their own learning and thinking. (p. 207)

Interestingly, the learning activities experienced during the institute were drawn from several different fields—mathematics, language arts, and science or social studies—so that participants would gain a broad understanding of constructivist learning.

The participants were then asked to consider the implications of their learning for pedagogy. "On Friday afternoon of each week, the group came together as a whole—a community of discourse—to propose and discuss pedagogical principles that were an outgrowth of the reflection on participants' own learning" (p. 208). Thus, in social constructivist manner, the cooperating teachers and student teachers worked together to develop and articulate an approach to learning and teaching.

INTEGRATION, INQUIRY, AND COMMUNITY: KEY COMPONENTS OF SOCIAL CONSTRUCTIVIST TEACHER EDUCATION

In this chapter, we have given an overview of social constructivism, illustrating it with reference to our own preservice program at OISE/UT and recent general developments in teacher education. By way of summary, we now wish to draw attention to three concepts that, in our view, are at the heart of social constructivism. These concepts will then provide a structure for a more detailed discussion in later chapters of how to build a social constructivist preservice program.

The first concept—*integration*—is central to social constructivism for several reasons. The close link in constructivism between knowledge and experience, theory and practice, demands an integrated program. Further, the holism of social constructivism—the connecting of various dimensions of life—calls for a program that advocates and models integration of the cognitive, social, emotional, and behavioral, the professional and the personal. And the inclusiveness of social constructivism requires a program that integrates mutual understanding and acceptance across all its aspects.

The second concept is *inquiry*. As we have seen, social constructivists maintain that all knowledge is subject to constant reassessment and critique, nothing being taken as fixed or absolute, as beyond examination and reconstruction. In particular, knowledge is open to individual and subgroup construction and interpretation. This necessitates having a preservice program that is nonauthoritarian, with an inquiry rather than a transmission orientation. Instructors can certainly help student teachers a great deal, but there must be constant dialogue and co-learning, with extensive opportunity for the students to reflect, give input, and develop their own ideas.

The third concept—*community*—is clearly essential to *social* constructivism. As indicated earlier, however, community has many dimensions: it is not just a matter of cooperative learning. It involves emotional expression, support, sharing, and inclusion. Sometimes in education we have concentrated largely on the sharing of *ideas*, on collaborative *learning*, on the *learning* community. But in our view, mutual support and other personal and emotional dimensions of community are also crucial for constructivist education. A preservice program that focuses exclusively on cognitive learning, whether carried out cooperatively or not, will not be very successful from a constructivist point of view. Students need strong support and a range of types of experiences as a basis for taking risks, developing innovative pedagogy, and giving personal meaning to what they are learning about teaching.

Our basic recommendation for preservice education, then, is to build a program that is integrated, inquiry-oriented, and community-based, these concepts being understood in social constructivist terms. In chapters 2, 3, and 4, respectively, we will discuss in detail the nature of these qualities and how to achieve them in a preservice program. We will do so largely by giving examples from a set of preservice programs we have studied in North America and Australia, as noted in the introduction. In chapter 5, we will argue that these three qualities are inseparable from an inclusive, equity-oriented approach, and we will illustrate how to build an inclusive preservice program by referring once again to actual programs, including those described in earlier chapters. In chapter 6, we will consider how to gain support for a social constructivist approach beyond one's own preservice program, in part to enable the survival and flourishing of one's program. In the final chapter we will discuss how to conduct ongoing self-study research on a preservice program, with a view to continual improvement of the program and modeling an inquiry approach for student teachers.

CHAPTER 2

Creating an Integrated
Preservice Program

Last year we began what we call Fabulous Friday, in which we attempt to integrate the day in the way a teacher would have an integrated day in a classroom, helping the student teachers understand that all the subject areas are related and that we're trying to teach the whole child rather than discrete subjects. That's the goal of the program as I see it.
—Joe Rafter, New York University preservice faculty member

In the previous chapter we identified integration, inquiry, and community as central themes of social constructivism. Here we will focus on the first theme, exploring in detail how to integrate a preservice program along social constructivist lines. Similar discussion of the other themes will follow in subsequent chapters. Among the integrative strategies we will consider here are: developing a shared philosophy, forming a collaborative faculty team, integrating campus courses, and connecting the campus program with the practicum.

Integration in a preservice program has many benefits from a social constructivist point of view. Student teachers learn to connect theory and practice; they see links between various dimensions of life and learning: the cognitive and the social, the academic and the personal, the professional and the everyday; and they develop a broad approach to teaching rather than acquiring disconnected pieces of knowledge and skill. Darling-Hammond and Macdonald (2000) in their study of the Bank Street preservice program report that a graduate of the program appreciated "the consistency of her experience in courses, advisement, and field experiences." The thorough grounding in child-centered pedagogy she received in this way now enables her to effectively evaluate individual students' learning, accommodate their differing needs, and support their growth (pp. 9–10).

THREE EXAMPLES OF INTEGRATED PROGRAMS

In describing the kind of integration we wish to advocate and strategies for achieving it, we will draw examples from three innovative preservice programs that we regard as social constructivist and that pay particular attention to integration. We will begin with a brief overview of the programs, providing more detail in later sections. It should be noted that these programs have many features in addition to the ones reviewed here: in particular, like all social constructivist programs, they place a heavy emphasis on inquiry and community as well as integration.

Because these programs actually exist, they show that integration in preservice education is feasible. However, a high level of integration is often difficult to achieve and may not be possible in all circumstances. At the end of the chapter we will describe some of the challenges to integration encountered even by these strong programs.

Bank Street's Elementary Master's Program

The elementary preservice master's program at Bank Street College of Education in New York City takes up to 4 years to complete, including part-time study, but the main field-experience year is done full-time, and integration of the program is most evident during this year. Usually about 40 student teachers are enrolled in the field-experience year, whether in early childhood education, childhood education, or a combination of the two. During this year students take a number of core courses and are in schools 3 days a week, in 3 or 4 successive placements.

According to Nancy Gropper, director of the program, a key factor in achieving integration is the advisory program. Each faculty member advises 5 to 7 student teachers, meeting weekly with them in a group session or "conference group" and individually on other occasions both on campus and in their practicum schools. While practice teaching is the central topic of the conference group meetings, advisors work hard to help the students understand the Bank Street general philosophy and apply it in their teaching. A second means of integrating the program is by appointing faculty who share the program philosophy: Gil Schmerler, who taught for some years in the elementary preservice program, stressed the role of the hiring process in ensuring consistency of outlook among faculty. Finally, considerable attention is given to relating the various courses to one another and ensuring consistency among different sections of the same course.

NYU's Undergraduate Program in Childhood Education

New York University's B.S. in childhood education is a 4-year, full-time undergraduate program with about 40 candidates in each of the third and fourth years. In her interview, Judith McVarish referred to it as an "integrated cohort program." The program in its present form was established in fall 2000, so at the time of our interviews in summer 2003, the first cohort had just completed their third year and some aspects of the program were still being worked out.

However, according to Frances Rust, director of the program, many of its key features had been tried out in earlier years, prior to the recent redesign.

Students take most of their foundations courses—for example, Inquiries into Teaching and Learning & Human Development—in the first and second years of the program, leaving the Curriculum & Instruction courses to the third and fourth years when most practice teaching is done. Students are in their placement 3 half days a week in the third year and 3 full days a week in the fourth year. This allows a close link to be forged between methods courses and practicum experiences. Each cohort in the third and fourth years also has classes together at the university from 8:30 to 4:00 every Friday, and it is during the Friday sessions that much of the integration of the campus program occurs. All faculty involved in the program attend a 2-hour planning meeting during the week and then the Friday session. Their respective contributions are brought together around themes, projects, and activities, with drama, music, and the arts melded into the day's experience.

Stanford University's Secondary Master's Program (STEP)

Stanford's secondary teacher education master's program runs for 12 months (June to June), with just 1 week between successive cohorts. It has an enrollment of about 60 to 75 student teachers. At the beginning of the program, all the students participate in a clinical experience in the summer program of a local middle school. Then they are given a student teaching placement, usually in one of the professional development schools associated with the program, where they remain throughout the academic year. The students are in their school placement for at least 20 hours a week, usually in the mornings; campus classes typically take place in the afternoons and evenings. The students specialize in one of 5 subject areas—mathematics, science, history/social science, English, or foreign language.

Integration of the program is a priority from the beginning. STEP director Rachel Lotan conducts an intensive orientation week with the new students in the summer, "building the cohort" and emphasizing key norms and principles of the program. This work is continued during the year. Linda Darling-Hammond, a senior professor and noted scholar in the field of teacher education, has ultimate responsibility for the direction and coherence of the program. She teaches STEP foundations courses in Adolescent Development and Principles of Learning, along with other faculty such as Amado Padillo and Roy Pea. Other senior faculty teaching foundations courses include Arnetha Ball (Literacies) and Ray McDermott (Equity and Democracy). The Curriculum & Instruction courses are taught by noted tenure-track faculty such as Jo Boaler, Pamela Grossman, and Sam Wineburg, in collaboration with doctoral students who have been teachers and are studying to become teacher educators and, in some cases, with other contract faculty who are practicing teachers. Considerable attention is paid to integrating the foundations and C&I courses with each other and with the practicum and ensuring that they embody the STEP philosophy. In the Practicum Seminar Rachel Lotan, assisted by Colin Haysman and others, connects the campus program with the practicum, using a range of activities to ensure that students have a common understanding of standards of practice and are implementing them in their teaching. Yvette Sarnowski, associate director for clinical work, also has a key integrative role as she selects appropriate schools and mentor teachers, works with supervisors, and generally oversees the practicum.

A SHARED, EXPLICIT PHILOSOPHY OF TEACHING AND LEARNING

A central means of integrating a preservice program is to have a shared philosophy of teaching and learning that is familiar to faculty, students, and field personnel. This facilitates connecting theory and practice since the same approach can be applied in different settings, notably in the various campus courses and the practicum. Further, it means that student teachers are aware of the intended approach and can critique and modify it rather than absorbing it unconsciously.

In the three programs we are highlighting, preservice staff spoke of the importance of being explicit about a program's goals and approach. For example, New York University's Joe Rafter stressed the need to be "transparent" with student teachers, constantly explaining that "this is what we're after, this is why we're doing this." And at Stanford, Ira Lit described how having frequent conversations with student teachers about "what we're doing and why we're doing it" models reflective practice and encourages students to adopt a similar approach in their own teaching.

A brief, written statement. The formulation of a program's philosophy may be quite brief. Indeed, an elaborate statement can be counterproductive, suggesting that the program has a precise, fixed direction. Linda Darling-Hammond (1997) has said of teaching in general that we need "medium grain" principles that are neither so general as to be meaningless nor so specific as to preclude initiative and choice (p. 229). In our view the same approach is applicable to preservice education.

Although a philosophy can be influential simply as part of the folklore of a program, there are advantages to having a written statement. It is useful to people who are as yet unfamiliar with the program, such as new instructors, beginning student teachers, and new mentor teachers. It can be incorporated into advertising, orientation material, and program handbooks. While greater depth of understanding is needed eventually, a written statement provides important initial direction.

Opportunities for discussion and revision. On a constructivist model, a program's philosophy should be subject to constant reinterpretation and modification by students and faculty alike, rather than regarded as a fixed, mandated position. Individual and subgroup differences in viewpoint, talent, interest, and circumstance must be accepted within the program: allowing and indeed encouraging such differences is a key principle of social constructivism. A program's philosophy should be a constant topic of conversation at retreats and in classes, the practicum, and other settings so faculty and students can come to a deep understanding of what it means, contribute to its revision, and achieve their own interpretations.

Ira Lit at Stanford noted that student teachers are aware of the STEP program's philosophy and also that it is open to modification; in class, they will say: "We know about this already; and we know that we're thinking and reflecting and revising." Further,

> they will push about "Why are we doing it this way?" or "What are we supposed to be getting out of this?" or "If you say we're supposed to be getting *x* and I'm not getting *x*, I'm going to tell you because you need to change what you do." And the faculty encourage that, because they want feedback and they want students to take ownership of their education.

Three examples of program philosophies. The philosophies of the programs we are citing in this chapter are outlined below as examples. We developed these composites largely on the basis of interviews with faculty but also with reference to documents on the programs. We present them here to give a sense of what may be included in a program's vision statement and how concise such a statement may be.

Bank Street Elementary Program

> Deweyan child-development approach
> attention to the whole child
> active learning
> flexibility, gentleness, and sensitivity
> inquiry
> close theory–practice connection
> classroom community
> collaboration
> equity and inclusion

NYU Childhood Education Program

> attending to the whole child
> integration of the curriculum
> importance of experience

reflection
broad approach to teaching that goes beyond particular subjects
lifelong learning
community
collaboration
equity and inclusion

Stanford Secondary Program

student-centeredness
student ownership
academic excellence
fostering pedagogical content knowledge
inquiry
theory–practice connection
broad approach to teaching
lifelong learning
collegiality and collaboration
equity and respect for diversity

Although these formulations are brief, the faculty we interviewed saw them as playing a key role in integrating and giving direction to the various aspects of their program. They had a clear sense of what their respective program philosophies meant and were able to explain and illustrate them in a variety of ways. An explicit philosophy, however, whether communicated orally or in writing, is just the tip of the iceberg. As important is the process whereby the meaning of the formulation is understood, reconstructed, and applied throughout the program.

A COLLABORATIVE FACULTY TEAM

Integration of a preservice program is increased if faculty work together as a team, building on the potential created by a shared philosophy. As noted, a social constructivist program's philosophy is subject to interpretation, and faculty need to develop interpretations jointly. This is often done in the context of solving problems, such as deciding what assignments to have in the campus program, which schools and mentor teachers to use, and whether to move a struggling student teacher to another placement. This does not mean that all team members will have the same point of view. However, by discussing issues together they will learn from each other, refine the program's approach, and reduce unproductive inconsistencies. We will now look at ways to foster a team approach in a preservice program.

A small program. Teamwork is easier if the program is relatively small, or is a subprogram within a larger one. This enables faculty to get to know one another, coordinate their activities, and engage in joint problem-solving. The three programs we are highlighting in this chapter are small, ranging from 60 to 75 students at Stanford to 40 in the core year(s) of both the NYU and Bank Street programs. Stanford has purposely limited its preservice enrollment (the recently added elementary program is also quite small); at NYU and Bank Street small size is achieved by dividing the substantial number of teacher education students among several subprograms. Although teamwork among faculty is possible in a large program, this requires extraordinary skills of leadership, administration, and community building that may not always be present. Teamwork and integration are simply more likely to occur in a smaller program.

Bank Street's Judy Leipzig, a former director of the elementary preservice program, commented on program size in her interview: "[A]lways smaller is better . . . [we value] that experience of knowing and being known, and having a small enough group so every voice can be heard." Later she said:

> Bank Street began as a small, intimate group of faculty who for many years engaged with each other in a way that is not necessarily typical, [and this] makes a difference. As new people come on board, there are enough long-time faculty here who greet them with the same sort of openness: "Here, look at my course outline. Let me mentor you about how you're going to teach a course for the first time that I have taught many times." . . . [And] advisors meet a minimum of once a month with their program director to talk about each student. . . . There's a culture of collaboration, [a sense] that you're not supposed to be in it alone.

Contract faculty integrated into the team. Small size by itself does not guarantee a close faculty team: community building within the team is also needed. A key move here is to involve all faculty—whether tenure-track or contract (including doctoral students)—as full members of the team. The three programs we are describing offer examples of these categories of staff working together with a high level of collaboration and mutual respect.

At Bank Street, regular faculty and contract staff plan and teach together. For example, there are multiple sections of the Mathematics and Reading courses and, according to Nancy Gropper, the regular faculty and adjuncts who teach the various sections get together regularly to refine them. At Stanford, each Curriculum & Instruction course is taught by a combined group of tenure-track faculty and contract instructors, the latter category including many advanced doctoral students who are former teachers and studying to become teacher educators. All members of the instructional team—tenure-track faculty, doctoral students, and other contract faculty—have prior K–12 teaching experience and are scholars of teacher education.

Linda Darling-Hammond commented that "the group operates as a team in terms of planning and implementing the program, and there is an egalitarian ethos." Colin Haysman, a full-time contract faculty member at Stanford, said that he felt valued and "not like a second-class citizen." Rachel Lotan described how she and two adjunct co-instructors plan and teach a course together. In Yvette Sarnowski's view, "the C&I professors are very good about co-teaching with practitioners; they often have several of their doctoral students—who are experienced teachers and sometimes also our practicum supervisors—working with them."

At NYU, tenure-track faculty work closely with "urban master teachers" (i.e., full-time appointees from the school system) and part-time adjunct instructors in the weekly planning meetings and the all-day Friday classes, resulting in a strong sense of camaraderie. The interviewees emphasized that the urban master teachers and adjuncts have key roles and are highly regarded, being preferred to any tenured faculty who do not share the goals of the program. Joe Rafter, an urban master teacher, commented:

> For the most part the urban master teachers have been very well accepted. . . . There are faculty who are very supportive of us. . . . I don't feel any animosity at all. In fact, in the cohort program I'm one of the leaders.

Planning and working together. Along with contract faculty, tenure-track faculty also need to work closely together so they become an integral part of the team. NYU program director Frances Rust noted that the whole team—contract and tenure-track alike—are involved in the all-day Friday sessions, and everyone has to attend the Tuesday planning meetings in the semesters in which they are teaching: "[T]hat's part of the deal. . . . I'm very strict about it." She has observed that as faculty plan and teach together they negotiate the approach to the program and their individual styles often change significantly. Judith McVarish, a tenure-track faculty member, observed:

> All the instructors in the cohort program met together [last year] for planning on Tuesdays for at least two hours, it would often go over. I was also there every Friday, for Friday instruction day. In the second semester, even though my Math course wasn't being taught, I stayed on with the planning group because I knew I would be involved the following year and I wanted to see the progression and where they were going.

At Bank Street, Gil Schmerler noted that "we have foundations study groups, with people who are teaching the foundations courses speaking with each other periodically; and child development groups working together." According to Helen Freidus, who taught in the elementary preservice program for several years, the final integrating project that is required of all Bank Street students can be assessed by any member of the faculty, and she personally recommends that her advisees work with someone else because she likes them to "have another perspective." She commented: "One of the big advantages [of this approach] is finding out what's going on in other courses and then trying to have your course either dovetail with or support what's going on." Judy Leipzig described the "cross-program home groups" at Bank Street in which faculty with similar concerns come together to investigate a particular aspect of the college's program. These groups meet sometimes during the monthly faculty meetings, sometimes outside these meetings. She said:

> [Such] growing together and coming together with people who might have slightly or very different perspectives has helped us all not only to learn about each other's perspectives but also to think in new ways.

Other team building activities. Apart from working together, a team can be strengthened through retreats, social events, email exchanges, and other more personal forms of interaction. For example, at NYU the new cohort program was planned in part at a week-long retreat; and every year the faculty team goes on a 3-day retreat. At Stanford, activities among the faculty include dinner parties in homes, with students present as well. Team building is also aided by the fact that several of the faculty who are full-time in STEP have their offices in the same area of the same university building. Yvette Sarnowski, after describing the team's very heavy workload, added: "But the good part is that Rachel and I and our staff are very supportive, and we take care of one another."

AN INTEGRATED CAMPUS PROGRAM

A further means of integration is to connect the various components of the campus program, so there actually *is* a program, as the University of Utah researchers put it (Arends & Winitzky, 1996). One might think that a social constructivist approach would require leaving it to the student teachers to integrate their experiences, since they could then develop their own synthesis suited to their distinctive needs and perspectives. However, in our view this would be asking too much of the students, who have such a brief period of preparation and are under intense pressure to do well in a climate often hostile to progressive approaches. As Fosnot (1996) says:

> Teacher education programs based on a constructivist view of learning need to do more than offer a constructivist perspective in a course or two. Teachers' beliefs need to be illuminated, discussed, and challenged. Teachers need to be engaged in learning experiences that confront traditional beliefs, in experiences where they can study children and their meaning-making, and in field experiences where they can experiment collaboratively. (p. 216)

This does not mean that students should be indoctrinated into a preset ideology of teaching and learning. But they should be co-inquirers with the faculty and each other, rather than having to go it alone. Paradoxically, they are more likely to construct their own, distinctive approach if they are supported by an integrated program and a sympathetic community than if they are left to "sink or swim."

Integration within courses. Two main types of course integration are needed: *within* courses and *across* courses. Special efforts to promote coherence within a course are required if different instructors teach different sections of the course, as is often the case. At Bank Street, Judy Leipzig noted that The Study of Children in Diverse and Inclusive Settings through Observation and Recording (O&R) is "one of our central integrating courses," and it is "flooded with child development" as is every other course in the college: "certain things are infused in every course." In order to ensure compatibility among different sections of O&R, it is jointly planned. Nancy Gropper reported:

> [T]his year I met with other course instructors who teach [O&R]; one of the co-chairs of the department brought us together as a group to have regular conversations about our work within that course . . . there are some differences [between sections] but there's a basic structure that is very much the same.

Helen Freidus described a similar process in relation to the Reading courses:

> In the Reading program, when I was co-chair, it was my mission to help us clarify and be more cohesive among our courses. You know, in literacy everybody bandies the terms about . . . so we've worked really hard (without becoming rigid) to share common meanings for the terms . . . making sure that what you mean by balanced literacy is what I mean by balanced literacy.

Rachel Lotan at Stanford observed that Adolescent Development is taught by 3 tenure-track faculty in separate sections of about 20 to 25 students each; however, the sections "have the same syllabus, the same readings, and the same final assignments, and the faculty meet every week to talk about their class." As described earlier, the Curriculum & Instruction courses at Stanford are taught by subject teams and considerable attention is given to integrating the contributions of the various team members. While the teams are led by outstanding tenure-track faculty, themselves scholars of teaching and former secondary teachers, the contract members (including doctoral students) also play a very significant role.

Integration across courses. Integration across courses obviously presents a greater challenge because of the range of fields and number of faculty involved. However, such integration is essential if student teachers are to develop a broad *approach* to teaching along social constructivist lines. Each course must help students to understand in greater depth the nature of this complex paradigm and to acquire the skills needed to implement it in their classroom. Having an integrated campus program also helps give students the support and encouragement they need to apply an innovative pedagogy in demanding practicum settings.

At Bank Street, integration across courses is furthered by hiring faculty who are committed to a progressive, child-centered philosophy. As Gil Schmerler said,

> [G]enerally people who come to Bank Street have a common enough understanding about the kind of pedagogy they believe in and a common enough style of interacting with students and other adults, so that there is consistency across the board.

Building on this foundation, there is continuing effort to help faculty deepen their understanding of the philosophy and apply it more fully in their courses. "There are constant new initiatives. People are looking at the problems as a whole, and where they see poor communication or articulation they create a group to get together and talk about things." Also, there is a set of core courses that help provide a coherent program:

> [E]verybody in the Department of Teacher Education has to take the O&R course . . . , Child Development, Developmental Variations in Language Acquisition, a foundations course [such as] Foundations of Modern Education or Principles & Problems in Education, Reading, Mathematics, Science, Arts or Music, and a curriculum course with social studies as the focus.

At Stanford, similarly, there are many core courses: Teaching in Heterogeneous Classrooms, Educating for Equity & Democracy, Adolescent Development & Learning, Principles of Learning for Teaching, Language Policies & Practices, the Centrality of Literacies in Teaching & Learning, and the Practicum Seminar. According to Linda Darling-Hammond, the tenure-track faculty who teach the foundations and C&I courses "do yeoman's duty" in STEP and "plan together as a team." The Practicum Seminar, taught primarily by Rachel Lotan as director but with the assistance of Colin Haysman and other faculty who teach specific topics, is designed to bring together various themes of the campus program and general topics such as assessment and special education. In addition, Rachel talks with instructors throughout the program about needed assignments and ensures that they are aware of each other's assignments; similarly, she talks with the students about the assignments and encourages them to integrate their project work across courses. In general, according to Ira Lit,

> it's pretty clear that it's a program; there is a philosophy and they work together as a cohort and the students see themselves as STEP students rather than, say, a math student who happens to be in teacher education. . . . [T]he students would probably tell you that some courses fit better than others . . . but overall they definitely see it as a program. . . . And the STEP

instructors are not just preparing teachers to be excellent at delivering content, which is a strong part of the program, but . . . there's a much broader idea. It's about being reflective and thoughtful about everything you do; it's more about an approach to teaching than a set of discrete skills.

At NYU, many subjects are integrated in the all-day Friday class: special education, health, math, science, social science, the arts, pedagogy, and teacher research. According to Frances Rust, this coherent approach to the campus program was adopted because many graduates of the former program "weren't really prepared for the complex workplace of the school . . . [and] didn't have a real sense of how to integrate the curriculum." In designing the new campus program, faculty from each curriculum area and from special education were brought together to ensure integration. In the first semester of implementing the program, members of the theatre education department were asked to help bring the many parts together, including dramatic arts, and were of enormous help. Then in the spring, music and visual arts were also incorporated into the Friday activities.

As this was the first year of the integrated cohort program at NYU, there were challenges; however, the interviewees felt it was already working well. Judith McVarish commented:

> Our ability to work together is getting better and better and less territorial. . . . Frances is a master at this. She is very patient yet firm and that's been a necessary component. We have an agenda and stick to it, and if somebody says, "Well I have to do this, this, and this," or "I need two hours for what I have to do, and it can't be in the afternoon," then we say, "Well let's look at what it is that we're doing and then see where all the pieces fit together." And very often people eventually see that it is okay if they don't get their two hours, and they see what they *are* getting [as a result of this approach].

She went on to describe how the integrated program is giving students greater awareness of the reality of teaching in schools:

> In my other [mathematics] course I have a whole week on graphing and data collection. . . . [But in the cohort program] it had a different feel to it: we'd have a graphing question for attendance each morning. So you're not talking about it in the same way. . . . The integrated program feels more like my fourth grade classroom, because that's how I took attendance and we'd have those kinds of discussions. . . . I didn't do graphing all in one week in the fourth grade, it was ongoing throughout the year.

CONNECTING THE CAMPUS PROGRAM
AND THE PRACTICUM

Faculty teamwork and course integration will be to little avail if the approach to teaching advocated at the university is incompatible with that found in the field placements. Such a gap leads student teachers to think that university faculty are out of touch with school realities and so to mistrust what they recommend; further, the students may feel too vulnerable in the practicum to follow a pedagogy different from that of their mentor teacher (Britzman, 1991). Students need a practicum setting conducive to honing their emerging social constructivist understandings and practices.

Not only should the practicum setting offer examples of constructivist pedagogy; the students' practicum experiences should also be a constant topic of conversation in the campus courses. It is inappropriate to leave students to make connections between constructivist theory and practice on their own. This is so because, as noted before, students feel vulnerable in the practicum; and also because they do not yet understand very clearly what constructivism is. We will now look at some conditions and strategies for linking the campus program and the practicum.

Practicum experiences spread or interspersed over the program.   One important condition for connecting the campus program and the practicum is to have field components throughout the preservice program, not just toward the end. Many writers have argued against the "theory first, practice later" approach that often characterizes preservice programs (Darling-Hammond, 1994; Wideen & Lemma, 1999). Constant opportunities are needed during the program to apply theory and reflect in and on practice. Tom (1997) is critical of programs where most teaching responsibility is "withheld until the end of the program," with professional knowledge "introduced prior to—and often separated from—teaching practice" (p. 143). Goodlad (1994) favors having "courses and field experiences blending into one and flowing into dominantly school-based activity accompanied by reflection" (p. 187).

In the three programs we are highlighting, as noted earlier, student teachers are in the practicum all or most days throughout their core education studies. At NYU and Bank Street they are in schools 3 days a week and at Stanford at least 20 hours a week. But even in programs where continuous school experience of this kind not possible, integration of theory and practice requires that practicum blocks occur at several points throughout the program.

Careful selection of mentor teachers and provision of professional development.   Another factor in integrating the campus program and the practicum is to select mentor teachers who are sympathetic to social constructivist pedagogy and then provide support for their growth in this approach. According to Schön (1987), "cooperating teachers are often casually selected because of availability, and too often lack essential knowledge and skills needed to strengthen the learning of prospective teachers" (p. 27). Some might think it presumptuous for preservice faculty to take strong initiative in choosing mentor teachers, but in our view it is essential. While tensions with school administrators and teachers may sometimes arise due to this approach, the well-being of the student teachers should be our first priority.

Just as important as selection of mentor teachers is their inservice development. Over time, teachers who were not initially very effective in their role can gain the necessary insights, attitudes, and skills. According to Borko and Mayfield (1995), preservice faculty need to work with mentor teachers to help them explore their assumptions and beliefs about their role and develop skills of providing feedback, active listening, and communication generally.

At Stanford, both Rachel Lotan as program director and Yvette Sarnowski as associate director for clinical work give a great deal of attention to the selection of mentor teachers. According to Rachel,

> Yvette is the one who establishes the relationships with the schools and the principals. . . . But I also go out because I like to see the classrooms; and we visit each and every person who is a potential cooperating teacher. . . . We don't just say, "Would you be interested in being a cooperating teacher?"

They also give priority to the ongoing development of mentor teachers. Yvette commented:

> I go into the classrooms of the student teachers and the cooperating teachers and work with the cooperating teachers. . . . [A]nd we always try to keep them informed about what our students are learning in their courses and attempting to implement in their practice, and why.

Tenure-track faculty also spend considerable time in the practicum schools and so are able to have significant impact on the mentors' teaching approach. Faculty from the program do workshops and coaching at the school site that all the teachers are free to utilize, and mentor teachers from partner schools are able to take professional courses at Stanford for a nominal fee. Furthermore, STEP faculty are involved in curriculum development, performance assessment development, and school restructuring efforts in several schools that are professional development school partners, two of which are new schools that were launched in partnership with the teacher education program. According to Linda Darling-Hammond,

> These efforts create considerable synergy between the school's efforts to build a learner-centered curriculum and the university's efforts to develop prospective teachers and veterans who can teach in the way such a curriculum demands.

At Bank Street, Gil Schmerler spoke of the great care with which mentor teachers are selected, and the college's insistence on retaining the right to make such decisions. He said that students are sent "to the teachers we know have been successful; occasionally we'll try someone new, who comes very highly recommended, but we're very quick to make sure that's working." Elsewhere in the interview he commented:

> I remember one principal saying "all my teachers are great" and my not believing that, because we had a very, very high standard of what a great cooperating teacher was . . . and it just seemed to me very obvious that you looked very carefully at each specific teacher, you went past the principal's word, you had all kinds of independent judgment, you looked yourself, and unless you were really clear that somebody was going to be great for your students you didn't consider them.

Selection and development of mentor teachers at Bank Street is facilitated by the intensive supervisory process, described earlier. As well as the individual and group meetings on campus, advisors spend half a day every 2 or 3 weeks in each advisee's classroom. In this way they hear and observe a great deal about the mentor teachers and the schools and so are in a strong position to select (and deselect) mentor teachers and share with them the program philosophy and expectations.

School partnerships and clustered placements. As we saw in chapter 1, integration of the campus program and the practicum is enhanced by building close relationships with partner schools and, as far as possible, clustering many student teachers in each school. This creates greater university presence in each school, increased opportunity for the development of mentor teachers, and peer support for student teachers during the practicum. It also facilitates supervision by faculty, since they can visit many students at once rather than constantly commuting around the district.

All three programs we are describing have taken steps toward close school partnerships and clustering student teachers in the practicum. At Stanford the interviewees described these efforts in some detail, and accordingly we will focus here on the STEP program. In her interview, Yvette Sarnowski explained the Stanford team's rationale for this approach:

> We have multiple reasons for wanting to cluster our student teachers. For one thing, our students really like the support of classmates in the school. For another, when they are discussing school issues in the cohort at the university . . . they can hear about the different cultures at different schools. . . . Something else we were finding was that students would have a really good individual mentor teacher, but when they went into the staffroom or a department meeting they would hear very disturbing things, and it was not a healthy environment. . . . So we were having students wondering whether they wanted to be teachers, or whether they could ever find a job in a school that would fit their philosophical belief system. . . . Then another issue is that, by infiltrating schools with a core number of teachers trying to make a change, we can actually help a school change existing practice; whereas if you are working with one teacher who is individually playing Don Quixote in a school, it goes nowhere.

Colin Haysman described Stanford's plans for more school partnerships in the future: "[The next big advance in our program] has to do with professional development schools: basing more of the work in a smaller number of schools; and we've already moved a lot on that. When I first came our students were in something like 50 different schools and now we're in 11 with the same number of students. And maybe that needs to come down to 5 or 6." Yvette Sarnowski noted that a major reason for her appointment to the program was to get to know the school districts and identify schools that, because they had a compatible philosophy and sufficient teachers interested in working as mentors, would make good PDSs. She remarked:

> [W]e want different types of experiences. So, for example, we have a cluster at East Palo Alto High School with 100 percent minority students, all students of color and from underprivileged families; and then we have another PDS partnership . . . with a pretty typical suburban California high school, with about 50/50 white and minority students.

Yvette went on to describe the typical process followed at Stanford in establishing PDSs:

> When we see a school that has teachers who use the kind of practice we like to see modeled for our students, and where the administration has a common vision of teaching for equity and excellence, then we talk about placing a few student teachers there. It may take 3 or 4 years before their faculty truly want to become a professional development school, but I have found that placing the seed of those student teachers, together with having enough cooperating teachers who really get into reflective practice and discussion of research in the field, means that pretty soon they ask us: "Well, could you come and help us?" . . . And we establish a formal agreement with the school; we don't pay them anything, but they get our professional services without charge. . . . Under the agreement, the school will take student teachers in classrooms where teachers are interested and model the practices we're hoping for, and we will support them in their identified professional development needs, do collaborative research with them, and do collaborative reflection on the preservice program. We help them in assessing where they would like to move and they give us a lot of feedback on how to improve our program.

Involving the same people on campus and in practicum schools. Integration of the campus program and the practicum is furthered if the same people are involved in both settings. In this way, ideas and community experience are brought from the campus into the practicum, and the practicum in turn impacts on the campus program. Supervisory staff who do not teach in the campus program often have difficulty representing the program in the field (Slick, 1998). Links are strengthened if the instructional staff make frequent visits to the practicum sites (Bullough & Gitlin, 1995; Ducharme & Ducharme, 1999; Tom, 1997).

At NYU, integration of the campus program and the field has been enhanced through the use of "urban master teachers." These are outstanding teachers on loan from the school system for a specified period to teach and supervise in the program. Joe Rafter observed that, while it is "a goal and a hope" to have more tenure-track faculty visiting practicum schools, in the meantime

> the different response to that concern taken by NYU is to hire urban master teachers, who are full-time faculty but not tenure track, and put them in the field so you have people with real school experience but also one foot in the university.

At Stanford, similarly, there are many people who participate in both settings. Tenure track faculty who teach the foundations and C&I courses are involved in a number of curriculum development, research, and school reform efforts in the schools where student teachers are clustered. Rachel Lotan and Yvette Sarnowski have major roles both on campus and in the field, and the doctoral students who help teach the C&I courses also do practicum supervision. Further, many mentor teachers from the practicum schools are involved in planning and team-teaching in campus courses.

Bank Street is renowned for its use of the same personnel in both settings, as described earlier. The central requirement of faculty in the program is that they do extensive practicum supervision; according to Gil Schmerler, their primary identity lies here. Judy Leipzig noted that apart from the weekly conference group on campus, "the advisor visits each student a minimum of every 3 weeks—and that really is a minimum—and spends the morning there looking at not just what the student teacher does but what's going on in the room, looking at individual children, thinking about the school, and thinking about this particular cooperating teacher. So that the advisor and the student really have a shared frame of reference."

Helen Freidus reported that the practicum conference group at Bank Street is intended as "an integrating experience" for the students' whole time in the program: "It is designed for students to have a forum for weaving together their coursework, their work in the field, and for sharing their conceptions and misconceptions with their colleagues." As described by Darling-Hammond and Macdonald (2000) in their study of the Bank Street program:

> Program directors and advisors balance administrative roles with teaching, advising, and recruitment, interviewing, selection, and ongoing mentoring of students. There is an institutional belief that participation in these different roles informs courses, advisement, and program decisions. Faculty who engage in field advisement learn the realities of schools and contribute directly to their improvement by taking their needs into consideration when teaching courses and advising students how to teach the children they both meet in the field placements. The involvement of directors in teaching, advisement, and supervision keeps them cognizant of the field and of the

kinds of placements where students experience exemplary teaching. Through direct engagement with the work of teaching and the work of schools, they learn what programs need to prepare teachers for. (pp. 18–19)

Meetings, seminars, and assignments linking the campus and the field. Another factor in integrating the campus and the field is activities and projects that cut across the two settings, such as meetings between faculty and practicum supervisors (Casey & Howson, 1993; Cole & Sorrill, 1992), practicum seminars with student teachers, and assignments that relate to both domains. In chapter 1 we discussed the conduct of action research projects by students during the practicum, with preparation and follow-up on campus (Clandinin, Davies, Hogan, & Kennard, 1993; Ross, 1987; Zeichner, 1996). Other projects linking the campus program and the practicum include reflection papers that use examples from the practicum, field-based journals, and in-class group assignments based on the practicum.

Faculty at NYU work closely with the practicum supervisors to increase their familiarity with the program philosophy and enhance their approach to practicum supervision. They also meet weekly with the student teachers in advisement groups to discuss their practicum experiences and relevant issues addressed in the campus program. Apart from scheduled activities of these kinds, there is a great deal of informal discussion of the practicum. Joe Rafter talked about his constant interaction with students regarding problems they face in the field, and Judith McVarish commented:

> Some of the students were out student teaching and wanted to know how to teach math, and so I would say: I'm here, I live here; come upstairs anytime. And I would give them things and we would sit and talk about what they were doing. . . . I think what is helpful for the students is that they know there's a community . . . and it's an ongoing, year-long thing. . . . In traditional methods classes, when math is over contact is often lost with the instructor.

At Bank Street, the conference groups ensure constant discussion of practicum experiences in the university campus setting in light of the program's philosophy. There are also frequent meetings among field supervisors to talk about the practicum work and particular student problems. And various projects cut across the two domains; for example, as described by Darling-Hammond and Macdonald (2000),

> The main assignment for the [O&R] course is an Individual Child Study for the purpose of "developing an increased awareness of the child's uniqueness, the relation of specific behavior to overall functioning, and the implications for learning." This document is developed over several months from a number of different assignments, including short weekly written observations of the child at school; a paper that examines the child in the context of his peers or group; an age-level study designed to see the child in light of developmental theory; and observations and interpretations of the child as a learner and member of a learning community. (p. 43)

This assignment is clearly in accord with the constructivist goal of bridging theory and practice. It explores fundamental themes of the campus program and has a major impact on student teachers' learning and effectiveness in the practicum.

At Stanford, Yvette Sarnowski said that when she was invited to join the program, she was told: "[W]hat we want is someone who can help us link the university to the field, the theory to the practice." She and Rachel Lotan meet every 3 or 4 weeks with the practicum supervisors, and are actually developing a whole curriculum for working with the supervisors. For example, they instruct the supervisors in how to support student teachers in negotiating California's new "teaching event assessment" of new teacher performance. "So Rachel and Colin teach them that in class, and then we teach the supervisors how to support it." Turning to formal courses, Rachel, Colin, and other contract staff work together in planning and teaching the weekly Practicum Seminar and then pass on much of the content to the practicum supervisors. They also help link the C&I courses with the rest of the program, including the practicum:

> We meet regularly with all the different instructors; they provide feedback and meet with some of the supervisors; we have a lead supervisor in each subject area who attends the C&I classes so they can give feedback to the other supervisors about what the students are learning in class that week.

MODELING AN INTEGRATED APPROACH TO LIFE AND LEARNING

Modeling is always important in teaching: show rather than tell, or show *and* tell (the approach we favor), are common phrases among teachers. It is especially important for a social constructivist approach because modeling is itself a manifestation of holism and integration: it links how we live with what we say. In this chapter, we have already indicated ways to model integration in a preservice program: through close collaboration within the faculty team, integration of the campus program, and connection of the campus program with the practicum. Here we address two additional areas in which we think modeling should occur. But first we note briefly the explicit advocacy of modeling among faculty we interviewed in the three programs.

The interviewees at NYU saw themselves as modeling, especially in their collaborative approach and program integration. Judith McVarish remarked: "[We had two coordinators for each cohort so that] it would convey a team approach, a collaborative approach, it would model that." Frances Rust described how they try to let the students see the complexities of collaborative teaching, partly through having student representation at the weekly planning meeting. "We want transparency. We want them to see that we're not always in agreement, that we often disagree about what we're doing, and that we're really planning." Similarly, Joe Rafter said that NYU's integrated, collaboratively taught program helps the students understand how a true learning community works:

> The students are able to see that we don't all necessarily agree with one another, and see the process of negotiating beliefs and attitudes and approaches to teaching. We're modeling what I hope they'll be able to get into when they go into schools, which is a sort of networking situation. So they won't be isolates teaching with their door shut. It's very important to reach out to people and get acknowledgment and collaborate with other people. That was how I became interested in teaching and satisfied with it.

At Bank Street the interviewees spoke of modeling, especially through their caring relationship with student teachers. Nancy Gropper said: "Because we are trying to prepare our students to address the individual needs of their students when they ultimately become teachers, we try to model that here." At Stanford, too, while the principles of the program are discussed explicitly with students, there is also a sense that they will learn through modeling by faculty of teamwork, a social emphasis, and care for students. For example, Ira Lit commented:

> [W]e are modeling collaborative work, and [the students] also have to do a lot of collaboration to try to build up that sensibility. . . . It's one thing to tell them they should be collaborative, but another for them to go into an institution where everybody goes into their own room and shuts the door. . . . They need to have some models and some experience of how to get out of that rut.

Connecting all aspects of life. An area of modeling that is needed from a social constructivist point of view is "holism" or the connection of all aspects of life. As we saw in Chapter 1, it is important for student teachers—during their program—to experience a holistic approach, connecting the professional with the personal and the academic with the social and emotional. The program should constantly model the insight that "we teach who we are," and accordingly that personal development and expression are of prime importance.

At Stanford there is modeling of links between various aspects of life, especially the professional, social, and personal. Ira Lit said:

> If somebody in the group is having a birthday, we all share a cake and sing happy birthday . . . and a lot of staff are working to support this. . . . [They] know the students incredibly well. They know what they are up to, what hurdles they face, and who is doing well where. . . . There is the weekly practicum seminar on Wednesdays and they all share pizza. Eating is a very communal experience and they do a lot of eating together.

Integration of various dimensions of life is seen at NYU, especially in the Fabulous Friday all-day class where the whole student cohort comes together, along with up to 10 faculty. Judith McVarish noted that the faculty originally planned to have two smaller cohorts, but "early on we put them together and . . . it was a fabulous group, and we wanted to develop that and maintain that community sense, so we had the whole group together from then on." The day begins with breakfast, which is a social occasion but one in which principles of nutrition are respected. Drama is also a key part of this day, along with art and music. Joe Rafter commented:

> There's commitment to the whole child. . . . [We want to prepare] teachers who are able to empathize with their students [rather than being] the mercenary who comes in from outside and works on the kids rather than with them.

In the Bank Street program, education of the whole child is at the center of the philosophy of teaching and learning. According to Nancy Gropper, "we're interested in preparing teachers to work with children in such a way that they recognize . . . the whole child, not just their academic development but also their social and emotional development and their physical development." This outlook is modeled especially in the conference groups, where students receive an enormous amount of support from their faculty advisors and from each other. Gil Schmerler reported:

> In every conference group I've had . . . there was a bonding . . . there's something about the conference group that brings people together. . . . [M]y sense is that there are an awful lot of emotional and social things going on in the groups. There are lots of tears and laughter and celebration and other things.

A caring, supportive teacher–student relationship. A specific dimension of a holistic approach, evidenced in all three programs, is a caring teacher–student relationship. Frances Rust at NYU reported that in the first and second years of the program there are "a core of advisors" who help support the students, and in the third and fourth years, "particularly with the all-day Friday program, we're so accessible to them. . . . [W]e know them in ways I have never known my students before . . . and since there are so many of us, they have a wealth of people to call on." Joe Rafter said:

> We have small advisory groups where we work closely with about 6 students and become aware of their demands and needs. . . . [This provides] an opportunity for them to talk to somebody and make clear their concerns or disappointments or whatever they have, and for us to give them emotional support.

Beyond these scheduled sessions, the faculty often meet with the students informally. Joe commented: "I see them here all the time. They're in my office every day, they just wander in. And they have things they're worried about, things they want to know about, some of the things I don't even have answers to but they want to come and talk to me."

At Stanford, a similar kind of caring is exhibited toward the student teachers. Rachel Lotan said: "I tell the students, 'It's not about seeing if you are survivors, like on TV; it's about creating an environment in which people are sane enough to be able to learn'." Linda Darling-Hammond commented: "The tenure-track faculty who work in STEP . . . know the students very well. . . . These folks, who are major researchers as well as full-time professors for doctoral and master's students, make time to attend students' portfolio hearings and often see them in the field as well." According to Colin Haysman,

> We have a low drop-out rate partly because of the amount of support they get in such a small cohort: everybody is known individually and everybody's needs are known. . . . If they are struggling there are innumerable people they can turn to: contract people helping within a particular course, people running the program like Rachel and myself who they know very well, their supervisor who sees them in school, and their mentor teacher.

Similarly, Yvette Sarnowski remarked: "Rachel and I spend a lot of our time talking to the students about things that have nothing to do with teaching but rather with how they are feeling about themselves. About 90 percent of them live on campus, many of them far from their families; and we become their family. . . . However, most of them also form very close bonds with their supervisors and their supervisory group peers, so there are 3 or 4 other people they can go to."

Nancy Gropper at Bank Street gets to know all the students well early on, both to assess their needs and so they feel they have someone they can come to:

> As program director, I interview everybody coming into the program with a few exceptions—sometimes another faculty member will do it—and I come to know each of these students at least initially and build a beginning relationship so that before they go into the supervised fieldwork they have somebody they can turn to. . . . I have multiple telephone and face-to-face conversations with them. . . . [And] I arrange the first placement for the fall. I have a conversation with every one of the students about . . . what age group and setting they want to start with, is there something in particular they are looking for, what are they looking to learn about in their first placement.

This sense of relationship is then developed even further with the faculty advisors in the conference groups. The students receive an enormous amount of support in the area where they need it most: the practicum. Helen Freidus referred to the conference group as "an emergent seminar that centers around needs and concerns." Judy Leipzig said of the conference group that it is a "very intimate, enduring, safe place." She also described the enormous amount of attention faculty give to students in the courses:

> Our courses are highly interactive and the teaching is often individualized. Many faculty include weekly dialogue journals of some sort that students hand in and instructors respond to individually. Many also have online

group conversations among students and between the students and the course instructor. All faculty encourage students to come meet with them, or to contact them, if they have any questions or problems, and if a student doesn't come, the course instructor is likely to contact both the student and the student's advisor to see if he/she can be of help. It is not uncommon for faculty and advisors to work together on behalf of a student. All faculty also work closely with the individual student whose work is not up to par, with the idea that we are more interested in the student acquiring the knowledge and skills she will need, than in having her prove to us that first time out the gate she is able to do the assignment at a high level. Many faculty have built into their courses the opportunity for students to hand in a piece of the final assignment so that they can be mentored while they are completing the assignment. Some faculty have built into their courses that they will meet with each student individually to plan for their final assignment for the course.

CHALLENGES TO INTEGRATION

Achieving integration in preservice education is not easy in universities and schools of education where discrete courses are the norm. According to Wood (1992), in the real world problems are always multifaceted, but this perspective is not widely shared in the educational arena. Indeed, integrated, collaborative approaches to teaching and research are frequently seen as less rigorous and less effective. Even student teachers sometimes wonder if they are learning optimally through this approach. Below are some of the specific challenges to integration noted by the faculty we interviewed.

Finding suitable staff. Because an integrated, social constructivist approach is unusual, finding faculty who will implement it is not always possible. Gil Schmerler noted that even at Bank Street, where hiring is done with an eye to appointing progressive staff, sometimes new faculty do not "instinctively pick up the Bank Street ethos," and as a result there is rebellion in their conference group. He added, however, that there is usually enough commonality of style to ensure consistency.

Judith McVarish at NYU reported difficulties with integrated course instruction due to faculty "not knowing how to do it differently . . . not accepting and believing that, if I let go of some of the things I have to teach, the students will still get important things." Similarly, Frances Rust observed that some faculty "have never taught with somebody else, and find it difficult to be on view to their colleagues." To a large extent, however, she saw this as a transitional phase. "[T]hey are starting to give on the colleague piece because the relationship with the students is so remarkable . . . and [also the approach] enhances their work with the students in the field because they know what the students are being taught."

Faculty workload. Program integration, especially in the early stages, can be very time-consuming; and the extra work involved is rarely recognized by the university or school of education. At Bank Street, Helen Freidus described the conference groups as "extremely labor intensive and extremely extensive." Similarly, Nancy Gropper commented:

> All the faculty seem to really love [the conference groups]. . . . [But] you know what it is to visit people in the field, it's very complicated, teachers have their own schedules and sometimes a faculty member will set up a visit with a student and then have to change it because a teacher feels it's not going to work out.

Judy Leipzig observed that the courses at Bank Street require a great deal of work because of the individual attention instructors give to students, as described in the previous section. She referred to instruction in the program as a complex and time-consuming process of "thinking together" with students about teaching and learning.

At Stanford, Rachel Lotan and Yvette Sarnowski mentioned the extraordinary time demands on them because of their duties on and off the campus and the work of pulling the various program components together. Ira Lit spoke in particular of the time pressures on tenure track faculty:

> All the [tenure track] faculty I know are working on the edge, they're pulled in so many directions. . . . And the pressure here . . . for junior faculty is exceptionally difficult. . . . Of course, the professional rewards are tremendous . . . but on the other hand, if you want to live a more balanced life it might not be the place to be.

Joe Rafter at NYU noted the time (and stress) involved in dealing with different personalities and getting all the instructors on board in a team-taught campus program. As his remarkable final statement revealed, however, he would not do it any other way:

> It's time consuming and mental energy consuming. But at the same time I think it's well worth it; I feel a certain elation when things work well. . . . It's just that we have a lot of commitments. Frances is amazing: I don't think she sleeps. . . . There are a million things that pull you in one direction or another, and the faculty meetings are endless. . . . But this is what I've aspired to all my life, and here I am.

Demanding students. While it is good to have preservice students who take charge of their learning, often they do not understand the institutional structure of universities, the demands on faculty, and the difficulty of implementing an integrated, constructivist program. They often have no idea what faculty do with themselves when they are not teaching campus classes or doing practicum supervision. At NYU, Judith McVarish reported that the students wanted her to be in class all the time:

It's difficult to get many staff to teach all those Fridays. . . . [For example] for me, if I teach a regular course here at the university, a 3-credit course, I can plan on my own, and I go into class a couple of hours 1 day a week. That's very different from spending 2 hours every Tuesday at the planning meeting and then all day Friday . . . and that's only one of the courses I'm required to teach. . . . So I sometimes didn't stay the entire Friday . . . and a few other people did that too. And the students didn't like that. . . . And my sense is we have to articulate this, and explain that in school too you will come in and out, you'll have a specialist who doesn't sit in your class all day. . . . There needs to be a way to fluidly move in and out and still maintain the continuity of a wholeness and a team approach.

Ira Lit at Stanford commented that the students are sometimes dissatisfied with attempts by faculty to promote a broader, integrated view of education, dealing with larger issues and long-term goals:

The students are very demanding, and they should be . . . if something is not working in a course you will know about it . . . and the faculty in STEP encourage that; they want feedback and they want the students to take ownership of their education. However, they also try to work with the students to see that there are broad, long-term outcomes. . . . That's a very difficult piece in teacher education: if you are trying to foster a long-term sensibility, how do you do that when people are in an immediate place and have very specific short-term needs? There's a lot of conversation with students about that.

Finding suitable schools and mentor teachers.   As we have discussed, a major aspect of program integration is connecting the campus courses to the practicum, and in particular establishing a social constructivist approach in both settings. However, a common problem, noted often in the research literature, is finding practicum schools and mentor teachers comfortable with the approach taken in the campus program. Interviewees in all three programs mentioned difficulties along these lines. Gil Schmerler at Bank Street commented that in some schools they have not found even one teacher whose approach truly matches that of the college, and in other cases the school administration has not been able to provide sufficient support. At NYU and Stanford similarly, while progress is now being made, it took several years to identify schools with which genuine partnership could be achieved.

Shortage of program time, especially in the current climate.   A social constructivist preservice program faces the challenge of finding time to explore integrated themes, especially given the current pressure from government agencies to "cover" a wide range of topics. In a sense this provides an argument *for* integration, since discrete coverage of all the required topics is clearly impossible; but no matter how one approaches the issue there is a difficulty. At NYU, for example, Frances Rust reported that while students are intrigued by the full-day integrated class on Fridays, they tend to be "resistant" to spending all that time on top of their other coursework and practicum commitments. They sometimes suggest the day could begin later and end earlier!

At Stanford, Rachel Lotan said that one of the strengths of the STEP program is the attention given to Curriculum & Instruction: a 3-hour class in the student's subject specialty every week for 3 quarters. And yet, she noted with some irony, "in the spring they say 'How come we don't have a C&I course?'!" Ira Lit observed:

> In California . . . the new content standards are so rigorous and demanding that it makes it difficult for the programs . . . to be attentive to the broader notion of teacher preparation. I don't think it's impossible, and we're doing this in STEP; but it makes it pretty daunting, and makes it more likely that programs will lean in the direction of the content standards and lose the bigger picture.

And Yvette Sarnowski remarked:

> We have too much to do in the amount of time available. . . . Students do in one year what is typically done by most human beings in two or three years. . . . So it's an overwhelming task we have given them, and therefore it's an overwhelming task for us to provide support for them. . . . And they are almost all high type-A personalities . . . they read all these case studies of really successful things and it doesn't work exactly that way, so then they come to see me and they're crying and saying maybe they shouldn't be teachers.

In the quotations in this section (and earlier ones), we see reference to many elements of a social constructivist approach to preservice education: concern for the larger picture, integrating different components of the program, a close teacher–student relationship, and academic and emotional support for students. However, we also see the challenges faced by those who would establish this approach under present circumstances. The cases studied in this chapter show that it is indeed possible to implement an integrated, constructivist approach in some instances. But clearly more resources and greater institutional support are required if the approach is to be achieved in more than a small number of preservice programs. We need solid commitment from schools of education and universities. Perhaps above all we need the appointment of program leaders, of the kind profiled in this chapter, who have the vision, ability, and specific mandate to bring the different elements together in a systematic, integrated manner.

CHAPTER 3

Fostering Inquiry in the Program

Of far more value than a collection of how-to's is the ability to study a situation, notice what students care about, what is important to them, and invent appropriate practices. . . . The goal of the program is to foster deliberative practice.

> —Lin Goodwin and Alexandria Lawrence,
> on the elementary preservice program
> at Teachers College, Columbia University,
> "A Professional Development School
> for Preparing Teachers for Urban Schools"

Inquiry by student teachers is central to social constructivist teacher education. Students critically assess prevailing educational ideas and practices (including their own) and construct a distinctive approach to teaching in dialogue with instructors and peers. Rather than passively receiving "expert" wisdom, they take ownership of their development. Because teaching and learning relate to one's whole way of life, their development as teachers has a major personal dimension, including self-discovery and self-assessment. The goal is for the student teachers to become lifelong learners, constantly inquiring into their beliefs and practices with respect to teaching and learning.

THREE EXAMPLES OF INQUIRY-ORIENTED PROGRAMS

In this chapter, we discuss the nature of an inquiry-oriented preservice program and describe ways of implementing such a program. In doing so, we provide concrete examples from three programs that are social constructivist in nature and have an inquiry emphasis. As in the previous chapter, we wish to stress that the three programs we present here have many features in addition to the one highlighted: our account of them is not exhaustive. In particular, like other programs featured in this book they embody integration and community to a high degree, as well as inquiry. We begin with a brief overview of the programs and then go on to systematic consideration of the components of an inquiry approach to teacher education.

The University of Sydney's Master of Teaching (MTeach)

The University of Sydney's MTeach is a 2-year, full-time program with both elementary and secondary streams. It is relatively large for a community-oriented, social constructivist program, having 250 student teachers in each year. A more intimate cohort experience is achieved in two main ways. First, the student body is divided into "Study One" groups of about 25 each, which meet weekly to study general pedagogy. These groups are normally team taught by 2 faculty facilitators, and as far as possible the same 2 instructors remain with the group over the 2 years. Second, another set of groups meet regularly to study a specific secondary teaching subject or, in the case of elementary candidates, a range of teaching subjects such as language arts and mathematics.

The MTeach program has been inquiry-oriented since its inception, having been established as part of a general movement at the University of Sydney toward case-based, problem-oriented professional programs (Ewing & Smith, 2002). According to David Smith, a key figure in establishing the program and director of the program from 2001 to 2003, there was growing recognition of the increased diversity and rapid change in society that required a new approach to teacher education. A societal perspective was lacking: "In my own teacher education, we never talked about parents or the community." Teaching had to become "as much a learning profession as a teaching profession," with a focus on one's own learning as well as student learning, and with greater attention to social justice issues.

Teachers College's M.A. in Elementary Education

The Master of Arts in elementary education at Teachers College, Columbia University may take up to 5 years to complete, including part-time study (although most complete it in 2 years). However, about 80 student teachers enroll annually in the field-experience year, which must be done full-time and is the heart of the program. During this year, the student teachers are in schools 3 1/2 days a week in two successive placements. They take a CORE course (so-called because it is seen as the core of the program) and a Models of Teaching course, which connect theory strongly to the practicum, and a Teaching Reading course that has close connections to CORE and Models and also to the practicum. The students are divided into 3 groups of about 25 for CORE, and each CORE group is again split into 2 smaller groups for an intensive weekly Student Teaching Seminar.

Emphasis on inquiry is one of the three "stances" of the program (and of teacher education generally at Teachers College). The others are social justice and "curriculum development" or acquiring a certain approach to teaching: a "repertoire of pedagogical strategies" rather than a "bag of tricks." These latter stances are also closely linked to inquiry as understood within social constructivism. According to Goodwin and Lawrence (2002) (Lin Goodwin is director of the Teachers College elementary program), the program is "[s]teeped in the philosophy of John Dewey and framed by a progressive tradition. . . . [It] emphasizes . . . the social construction of knowledge, teacher decision making and reflection, and teaching as a moral and political endeavor" (p. 69). Following Dewey (1929/1960, p. 15), the program focuses on "personal illumination and liberation" rather than "how to's." "We avoid prescription from the outset, believing that our students should be exposed to and should critique many perspectives on teaching," identifying and refining their own perspective (Goodwin & Lawrence, 2002, p. 76).

OISE/UT's Mid-Town Bachelor of Education

At OISE/UT, the elementary post-baccalaureate B.Ed. program involves 9 months of full-time study. The roughly 600 students in the program are divided into 9 cohorts, each with its faculty team and somewhat distinctive program. The Mid-Town cohort program in which we (the authors) teach enrolls approximately 65 candidates each year. It is called Mid-Town because of the location of its practicum schools in Toronto's multiracial, multiethnic urban core. The faculty team consists of the 2 coordinators, who are "seconded" (i.e., on loan) full-time from school boards; 2 tenured faculty (ourselves) who are part-time in the program, having other duties in the school of education; and 2 or 3 part-time contract instructors (the number varies from year to year).

The Mid-Town program has an explicit inquiry philosophy. The first item in its vision statement is Teachers as Thoughtful Practitioners, which is elaborated as follows: "Student teachers are respected as thoughtful professionals, growing in the knowledge and abilities needed to meet the challenges of contemporary schools. As future teachers, they are encouraged to see themselves as having a central role in schooling. Their theories, experiences, insights, and interests are incorporated into the program." Another item in the vision statement is Action Research Focus, explained as follows: "We define action research as inquiry by participants into their own practice with a view to understanding and improvement. Such research is central to our program."

We turn now to a discussion of the nature of an inquiry-oriented preservice program and the complex process involved in moving in that direction. Having student teachers complete 1 or 2 research projects is not sufficient. The whole program has to have a strong inquiry emphasis so students come to understand in depth what the approach is and feel supported in pursuing it in both the campus program and the practicum. This in turn requires that certain conditions are in place: a supportive program, an integrated program emphasizing inquiry throughout, connections between theory and practice, and a nonauthoritarian approach.

A SUPPORTIVE PROGRAM

Support from peers. If student teachers are to inquire into their own educational ideas and practices, they have to feel supported by their peers in the program community. They need to have a sense of security and a personal bond with each other so they are willing to work together in collaborative projects, take risks in class discussions, and bring their personal lives and experiences into the dialogue. They also need peer support in their practicum placements as they attempt to hone an innovative pedagogy.

At the University of Sydney, a sense of community is found even in the total year group of 250, and activities at this level occur every week. However, the main peer support comes from the Study One general curriculum groups of about 25; the subject area groups, which are also small but vary in size; and the clusters of student teachers in their practicum placements. With respect to the elementary subject-oriented groups Robyn Ewing, co-director of the program, noted:

> The 75 elementary students are divided into 3 groups for their curriculum work, and they develop a very strong interconnection with people in their group. . . . [T]here's a lot of community building . . . and collaborative activity to get them to develop together as a group and take responsibility for themselves and each other, making sure that the group is functioning and everyone is participating and contributing. We use Jig-Saw groups, Think-Pair-Share activities, and presentations in small groups; and we discuss the meaning of communication and how people communicate. The students look at a case together and present the issues from the case . . . to the whole group.

Speaking of the secondary subject area groups, Paul Dufficy said:

> In the specialized secondary subject areas [the groups] have worked really well because they form strong relationships. . . . [I]t gives the opportunity for classrooms to be quite productive places because [with the older MTeach intake] there is a fair bit of stuff they have already worked through in their own lives, so they are ready to go and they are very supportive of each other.

At Teachers College, similarly, the elementary program emphasizes community building in order to strengthen inquiry. Various types and sizes of groupings are used. According to Anne Sabatini, apart from whole-cohort activities from time to time, "I mix them up in the Models of Teaching course . . . so they get to know different people; and in their teaching assignments, where they are in two different schools . . . during the year, they get to know different classmates." And in the CORE groups of 25 and the Teaching Reading groups they become quite close because they are together for the whole year. She commented: "We want to provide teacher education in a community setting where people learn from each other . . . we do not want to create that isolated feeling of everybody on his or her own."

Michele Genor at Teachers College stressed the importance of clustering students in the partner schools, saying that they hope in future to do this to an even greater extent so the relationship with the schools will be strengthened and students will have more peer support during in the practicum. She explained in general the role of community in supporting inquiry in the program: "[I]f they have a sense of trust they can talk about the issues and the challenges they are facing in classrooms. Trust allows them to move beyond just sharing to actually looking to one another for help in reflection and examination, and then continually challenging the insight that comes from this examination. . . . There is a lot of disrupting of assumptions, talking them through for the first time; so we work hard to nurture a place where that can happen." She believes this has paid off:

> They have become very close this year, and there's an attitude—and we say this from the first day—that the people in this room are the only people who know really what you're going through. You may have spouses, you may have partners, you may have parents who really won't "get it" because they're not in it, they're not trying to juggle everything you are. . . . [M]any of our graduates work in our partner schools, and [I have observed that] there are groups of graduates who are very connected and use each other as resources and mentors.

In the OISE/UT Mid-Town program, too, strong peer relationships are fostered as a way of supporting inquiry. A general tone of community and mutual support is established through the introductory material sent to accepted applicants and at "Options Night" in the spring when in-coming candidates select a particular cohort program. After they have chosen Mid-Town we send them a welcoming letter, emphasizing again the community dimension of the program. Then follow community building activities during the first week, an overnight retreat early in the term, getting-to-know-you activities and collaborative work in regular classes, and frequent social events. Usually the cohort is split into 2 smaller groups for classes so students have more opportunity to express their views and get to know one another; and mixed groupings are used, both on campus and in the schools, so the whole cohort becomes a community. When we visit a practicum school we meet with the student teachers both individually and as a group, encouraging them to share with each other and support each other.

Research on the Mid-Town program has shown that the community experience enhances inquiry (Beck & Kosnik, 2001; Kosnik & Beck, 2003). For example, student teachers are willing to share their queries and concerns to a considerable degree. We suggested to one student who was having difficulty with classroom management that he talk about the problem with other Mid-Town students at the same school. By the time we visited him again, he had discussed it with all 8 fellow students and 3 mentor teachers as well! As a result he became aware of several new strategies and his classroom management difficulties decreased. Another student, in an interview toward the end of the year, commented:

> The program has helped me because the individual encouragement has been very, very positive; just the support, knowing the support is there. . . . That has been encouraging and has brought out my best results. . . . I'm going to make sure I'm networking when I get out there [as a teacher]. I want to meet up with other teachers and say, How can we meet the expectations together?

Support from faculty. Apart from peer support, student teachers need a supportive relationship with faculty if they are to adopt an inquiry approach to teaching. After a lifetime of transmission education (Lortie, 1975) such an approach is frightening to many student teachers. Especially with the current emphasis on transmission teaching in school systems, they wonder how they will survive as teachers if they do not take that route. They need a connection with faculty who clearly believe in an inquiry approach and who show by their words and actions that they will back them up in developing this approach, both on the university campus and in the practicum.

In the Teachers College program, the faculty get to know the students well and develop a close relationship with them. According to Michele Genor, this enables faculty to support the students and even move beyond support and push for deep critical reflection. Catherine Pangan observed that the faculty discuss what is happening in the practicum at their Tuesday CORE meetings, and also at their biweekly meetings with practicum supervisors. As a result, "you can discuss a student freely and keep track of their progress while sharing support strategies from around the table." Similarly, Anne Sabatini said:

> [B]y the time the term is over, every student has been discussed in some way, shape or form. . . . It's a kind of triangulation: you get some impressions from the supervisors, some (in my case) from the Models of Teaching class, and some from the CORE faculty and instructors, as to who these people are essentially and any concerns and possible solutions.

Apart from getting to know the students and monitoring their progress, faculty work to ensure that the students are supported in an inquiry approach in the practicum. Practicum supervisors are carefully selected and then constantly updated in a bimonthly meeting where there is discussion of the developing principles, goals, and activities of the program.

In the Mid-Town program faculty participate in the cohort community, getting to know the students and taking an interest in them at a personal as well as a professional level. One student in a fall interview said: "I'm finding the program fantastic because it's so supportive. There's never one law, there's never a right way or a wrong way, and if we have any questions we can always come to you. I just feel it's a very nurturing environment." Another commented: "I love the fact that you guys never treat us like kids, that you respect our opinions. I really feel when I'm talking you're listening, not just other students but the teachers are listening. I can say what I think without feeling that the faculty are going to get defensive; which is a really nice environment because it's so rare."

In the practicum in particular we support the student teachers. All practicum supervision is done by the faculty team themselves, so the students feel well protected. This also means we have direct impact on the mentor teachers in terms of their approach to teaching and to mentoring our students. We are careful in choice of mentor teachers, taking charge of selection (and deselection) ourselves rather than leaving it to superintendents and principals or even to the practicum office. Where a practicum is not working out we often move the student, calling on other team members to help find a more suitable placement. If a student is not moved but has a difficult first placement through no fault of his or her own, we make sure the second one is with a particularly supportive and innovative mentor.

AN INTEGRATED PROGRAM

Support from peers and faculty, while very important for inquiry, is not sufficient. All aspects of the program must work together to reinforce an inquiry approach. There is a paradox here, as noted in chapter 1, in that systematically promoting a particular approach might suggest a degree of control and conformity, whereas inquiry should be allowed to go wherever it leads. But while students must ultimately decide which pedagogy to adopt, they need a comprehensive introduction to inquiry in order to understand what it is. Students have extensive knowledge of transmission education; the time has come for them see in detail the nature and rationale of an inquiry approach, while being free to make up their own minds.

At Teachers University, the CORE and Models of Teaching (and Teaching Reading) courses present a consistent inquiry approach to curriculum and teaching. Goodwin and Lawrence (2002) state:

> What distinguishes the experience [in the Teachers College elementary program] from a simple progression of courses plus field experience is the preservice CORE which integrates curriculum and instruction in elementary schools, curriculum design, social studies methods, and models of teaching. . . . The preservice CORE is the heart and the identity of the program. (p. 71)

The integration of the program is especially evident for those students whose practicum is in one of the program's professional development schools. Ivonne Torres, a teacher at one of the PDSs and a clinical instructor in the program, commented: "[A]t my school, where they do their student teaching placement, it's great to have someone who has that link to the University. It gives continuity, it links it even more closely. . . . I attend the staff meetings every Tuesday and am very much informed . . . and have a lot of input into decisions." Joint research between program faculty and mentor teachers also occurs in the PDS sites, serving to integrate the program further (Goodwin & Lawrence, 2002).

There is constant activity at Teachers College to ensure that the goal of an integrated, inquiry-oriented program becomes a reality. Catherine Pangan commented on the extent of the planning and implementation work: first the faculty meet, then the whole team, every week throughout the year, including the summer. Michele Genor said:

> We all plan and enact the weekly CORE class together, and then we take all this information and continually share it with all those involved in the program. We have a very successful and collaborative system of communication in place that translates into responsive support of our students.

According to Goodwin and Lawrence (2002), the purpose of this weekly planning is to foster "constant reflection about the enactment of standards . . . explicit discussions about what we are doing and why," in order to "align philosophy with practice" (p. 82).

At the University of Sydney, similarly, every aspect of the program is carefully planned to enable students to understand and acquire an inquiry approach. Paul Dufficy remarked:

> [W]hat I am thinking through in my work is how I can assist young people to become good ESL teachers in such a way that the processes I use in doing that are the same as the processes they can use to assist kids to become good mathematicians or whatever, and also the same ones that mentor teachers can use to assist young people to become teachers.

Study One is designed to further this goal in a systematic way. David Smith described how Study One emphasizes "non-subject-specific issues" and "concepts of curriculum," rather than focusing on "specific subject areas."

> We look at the different contexts in which curriculum is used, its nature and characteristics, models of curriculum development, evaluation and assessment, the whole context of outcomes-based education in our state system: what it means, where does it come from, how does one work with this approach. We look at issues of curriculum and educational change, organizational change, and policy issues having to do with gender, antidiscrimination, job protection, environmental education across the curriculum, integrated curriculum . . . trying to look across or beyond or beneath subject areas and raise questions that usually don't get raised when you just start with specific subjects.

Apart from planning such a program, steps are taken (as at Teachers College) to ensure that the plans are consistently implemented (Ewing & Smith,

2002). This begins with attempting (as far as possible) to bring faculty into the program who are committed to such an approach. David Smith said: "[We try] to screen the staff who teach in the program. . . . [T]here are certain things that underpin the MTeach and if someone is not committed to those, or wants to undermine them, then they shouldn't be involved in the program." Once the faculty have been selected, every effort is then made to get the whole team onboard. Robyn Ewing reported: "We have tried this year . . . to be much more explicit in the course outline about the team building activities that are so important at the beginning of Study One." And David commented:

> We ran a very strong professional development program in the 12 months before the program began . . . in which we looked at what it means to run an inquiry-based, case-based, problem-based approach to teaching. . . . [And now] we run professional development programs every semester, sometimes a couple of times a semester . . . there is always professional development for new staff . . . [and] we try to have social occasions such as a lunch about twice a semester, around some topic, or a professional development day.

CONNECTING THEORY AND PRACTICE

From a social constructivist perspective, inquiry involves movement back and forth between theory and practice: neither can be developed effectively without the other. An inquiry-oriented preservice program, then, has to deal constantly with questions of practice as well as theory, linking the campus program closely with the practicum. Only in this way will student teachers acquire a deep interest in theory and become reflective, critical practitioners.

In Sydney's MTeach program, curriculum theory is considered in the context of practical issues and examples (Ewing & Smith, 2002). According to David Smith, in Study One small groups of student teachers work cooperatively over the 2 years in an inquiry-oriented way, grappling with "real cases or real issues concerned with what goes on in schools and classrooms." Robyn Ewing referred to the case-based approach as "the basis of everything," "the heart of what we do across the board" in the program. She said that in order to strengthen the program they are working to extend the variety of cases studied. The cases used so far have tended to focus on critical (i.e., rather unusual) incidents, whereas they are now adding ones that look at "the everydayness and nitty-gritty of teaching."

The final 10-week internship in year 2 of the MTeach is meant to be a time when the theory and practice of the program come together fully, thus providing a bridge between the preservice experience and full-time teaching. At this stage the candidates have obtained their teacher accreditation and so can take full responsibility in the classroom. However, instead of turning the class over to them entirely, as happens in many internships, they only teach about two-thirds of the time (Ewing & Smith, 2002) and so are able to maintain a strong inquiry orientation. They are expected to not only do an action research project (to be described later) but also continue to develop a critical, innovative approach in general. The carefully selected mentor teachers also have additional time (because of the presence of the interns), and this enables them to model and discuss how a reflective approach can be implemented in practice. Robyn Ewing commented: "We want the mentors to act as critical friends, making their tacit knowledge explicit to their interns."

In the Mid-Town program at OISE/UT, the connection between theory and practice is achieved in part by involving all faculty in practicum supervision. In this way, faculty see firsthand what is going on in the partner schools and are able to bring examples from these settings to their campus classes. Further, it is our policy to combine theory and practice in all courses, even foundations courses. Practical techniques are theorized and general principles are illustrated with practical examples. As a result, it becomes clear to students that both the theory and practice of teaching are constantly open to modification, interpretation, and refinement: practice is not just an application of preset theory.

At Teachers College, the full-time field experience year is aimed specifically at maximizing links between theory and practice, with a view to promoting an inquiry approach to teaching. The practicum takes place throughout the year and dovetails with the campus program. Catherine Pangan commented: "Most [preservice programs] separate the student teaching and the coursework, and ours is unusual because we have the coursework and the student teaching together." According to Anne Sabatini, although students "have up to 5 years to finish the program . . . an absolute must is [to take] a set of courses . . . while they are student teaching, because we discuss the relationship [between the two]. . . . [W]hen they student teach, they have to do CORE, Teaching Reading, and Models of Teaching."

Michele Genor reported that there is a great deal of discussion of the practicum in CORE, Models, and Teaching Reading, and that the Practicum Seminar (which is part of the weekly CORE session) gives students "an opportunity to talk about their placements . . . attempting to make the connection between CORE and what is going on in their classroom." Further, within each course, theory is approached in such a way as to underscore its connection with practice. In CORE, for example, what is being considered is not just social studies methods but a general approach to teaching. The success of these efforts was noted by Ivonne Torres:

> It's a program that has . . . attempted to merge theory and practice, and I
> think it has been very successful. The program has aligned what the student
> teachers are facing at a given time of the year with the content of the class.
> There's a lot of thought behind the readings, the articles and books that are
> chosen.

Goodwin and Lawrence (2002) state that the CORE course explores questions such as: "What do children need? How do we know what children need (and by whose authority do we derive that knowledge)? How do we organize instruction to address children's needs in the classroom?" This inquiry in turn leads into topics such as "child development, lesson planning, management, organization of the learning environment, and understanding classroom and school communities" (p. 71).

The Practicum Seminar at Teachers College plays a particularly important role in relating theory to the practicum. For the third hour of the weekly CORE class, each CORE cohort splits into two subgroups of about a dozen students under the leadership of a contract faculty member with substantial background in teaching. According to Catherine Pangan, in this Practicum Seminar,

> we get into the nitty-gritty practical things, like if a student is doing such and such in my class, what are some ways to solve the problem? And with 12 other students going through the same thing, plus an experienced teacher, [they can get help]. So theory is related to practice and all kinds of pedagogical explanations are discussed.

A NONAUTHORITARIAN APPROACH

In order to foster inquiry, a nonauthoritarian atmosphere should pervade the program. In accordance with the social constructivist paradigm, students must feel free to reach their own conclusions and adopt their own teaching strategies. While we may systematically advocate an inquiry approach, as discussed earlier, our advocacy should not take an authoritarian form. We have to listen closely to our students and be open and respectful toward their opinions; and our own view of what constitutes an inquiry approach should be flexible and subject to change.

The faculty in Sydney's MTeach program work hard to ensure that students are respected and given ownership of their learning. This was part of the conception of the program when it was established. As David Smith said:

> [We could see that] the knowledge base of teaching had increased enormously. The whole idea that somehow in 12 months you could prepare a young person to teach had become highly problematic. . . . So we decided first of all to reduce the amount of face-to-face teaching we would do, and . . . help them become the most effective learners they could be . . . giving the students much more say in decision making about the way they construct their learning together and their work with one another, particularly in Study One. Also we decided to use criterion-based assessment rather than simple grading.

Similarly, Robyn Ewing spoke of the need for co-research, and of the importance of honoring students' personal experience through "mediated reflection" based on journal entries. Paul Dufficy reported coming to the conclusion that large lectures should only be used occasionally since, over time, they affect the quality of our teaching; they do not "assist people to become teachers" but rather model a transmission approach.

At Teachers College there was a similar drive to reduce class size. Anne Sabatini noted that while some faculty were able to handle large classes by breaking them up for small group activities, the students wanted a closer relationship with faculty. Along with smaller classes, there is now greater emphasis on student initiative and choice. Anne commented:

> I allow plenty of latitude for the group to assign their own tasks. . . . I teach them how to work in dyads and triads. . . . I get to know them well, and they get to know each other well. . . . I feel that in preparing teachers for today's schools, it has to be this kind of model.

To accentuate the personal nature of their inquiry into teaching, students at the beginning of the program are asked to write an autobiography "that becomes a lens for consciously examining one's attitudes and expectations about schools, children, and teaching. Such an examination exposes students' preconceptions to self-critique and encourages them to develop new ways of thinking and acting that are related to personal knowledge" (Goodwin & Lawrence, 2002, p. 79). Throughout the year, students continue this inquiry by keeping a journal and discussing it constantly with their supervisors; the purpose of this activity is "to develop [their] skills as deliberative, reflective teachers" (p. 79).

In the Mid-Town program, we attempt to create a context in which students feel free to disagree, be critical, and present their own views. Through social interaction and other means we try to reduce the distance between us as much as possible. As mentioned earlier, we divide the cohort into 2 sections for most classes and use small group work so students have an opportunity to say what they think. We listen carefully to their opinions and draw attention to shifts in our views that result from their input. We emphasize the theory and practice of dialogical teaching and teachers and students learning together.

As a component of this approach, we do extensive research on the program and involve our students as survey respondents and interviewees. Sometimes we invite them to assist in designing the research, especially with respect to which issues should be explored and which specific questions would be effective in eliciting information. We then share the findings of the research with them and detail the changes made to the program as a result of the research.

In interviews, Mid-Town students have expressed appreciation of these efforts and noted the impact on their development (Beck & Kosnik, 2001; Kosnik & Beck, 2003). For example, Rebecca said: "You can be who you are [in Mid-Town] and people will accept you for who you are." Heather commented: "I like what we're doing because it allows us to be the type of teachers we are each most adept to become. I feel we are really being encouraged to experiment as teachers, explore methods, explore possibilities, and just develop into individual teachers." Catherine said: "I find all the instructors very informative, but it's not an 'I know everything and I'm going to tell you everything' approach. Rather it's 'I'm going to share this with you'." She gave a specific example:

> Clive gave us this paper to read on teacher development and I thought it was the most derogatory, mean, nasty paper I've ever read. It totally insulted the entire room of preservice teachers. . . . So I put up my hand, I was the first person to speak out. I said, "I've been dying for a week to talk to you about this paper. This is the dumbest paper." And he just let us cut it to bits. It's wonderful. He didn't say, this is why I made you read it. . . . His reaction was totally just, okay, they hated it.

RESEARCH PROJECTS BY STUDENT TEACHERS

We turn now specifically to research projects conducted by student teachers within a preservice program. These often take the form of "action research" (Kosnik & Beck, 2000; Ross, 1987; Zeichner, 1996), by which we mean research that is designed to improve practice as well as enhance understanding, and that involves cycles of assessment/observation, theorizing, program modification, and further assessment/observation. However, many kinds of research are beneficial in teaching and hence appropriate in a teacher education program.

As noted in chapter 1, Ross (1987) has found that new teachers often do not continue to do research in a formal way after graduation, especially in the difficult first few years of teaching. In her view, then, a principal reason for having students do such research in the program is to help them see teaching "as a process that involves inquiry and experimentation" (p. 131). Along with this aim, however, we believe that research by student teachers is important to give them familiarity with the theory and practice of teacher research and a favorable attitude toward it. One of our goals should be that many of them, at least, will eventually go on to do teacher research in their own classroom.

In the Sydney MTeach program a collaborative research project is conducted by the students in the first term of year 2. Part of the purpose of this project is to help students acquire research skills for use in their main action research project, which comes later. Students work in groups of about 4 "to participate in, investigate, reflect and report upon, both orally and in poster form, some aspect of the relationship between community and school, at either the macro or micro level" (quoted from course materials). The investigation may, for example, be of a school council, a community agency with close links to schools, or an interaction between school and community personnel. The poster and presentation include: a rationale for the investigation; a brief description of the community/school context; a brief account of the methodology; results; conclusions and educational implications; and an annotated bibliography of relevant literature. After presentations within each Study One class, the posters are put on display in the school of education.

The major research assignment in the MTeach is the action research project, done during the 10-week internship in the second term of year 2 (Ewing & Smith, 2002). The topic of each project is negotiated with the relevant partnership school, often with an eye to benefiting the school; however, the primary purpose of the research is improvement of the new teacher's own practice. The research may involve, for example, assessing particular strategies of classroom management, developing ways of facilitating student discussion, experimenting with various assessment methods, or improving skills of explaining or demonstrating. The final report must include: an outline of why it was important to bring about change, an indication of the changes attempted, the action research cycles undertaken (including strategies used, data gathered, and results achieved), a critical discussion of the results and the changes brought about, and a critically reflective comment on the research, its process, and its results. The final requirement is to present a report of the research to peers and faculty in a poster session at the post-internship conference.

The OISE/UT Mid-Town program, like the Sydney MTeach, has an earlier preparatory research assignment called "Prep Steps." We developed this assignment relatively recently to help reduce some of the mystique and even fear surrounding the main action research project. While in our view it is important to use the word "research" to refer to certain program assignments (in order to show students that they can do research, and that it is valuable), we had noticed that the term often made students quite apprehensive. In the Prep Steps project, done during the first practicum, the students observe in their classroom; interview their mentor teacher; identify an issue or opportunity in the class; survey their students and briefly interview a few of them about the matter in question (e.g., how they feel about physical education, what kind of novels they like to read, what math activities they find helpful); and then devise 3 program modifications suggested by the research (without necessarily implementing them). The report is written up in stages and is only about 8 pages long. The students find this project quite manageable and are impressed by how much they learn, especially from the pupil interviews; as a result, their fear of the upcoming second-semester project largely evaporates.

The main action research project, conducted in the second semester, begins in the same way as Prep Steps but in a new school placement and usually focused on a different topic. Three new components are added: implementing program changes; assessing their effectiveness; and writing a reflection on the total experience. Because the process is longer, the research begins early in the semester during the weekly STEP (Student Teacher Experience Program) visits that precede the practice teaching block. Some of the reflection activities are done as in-class group work back at the campus. As with Prep Steps, the students generally value the research and learn a considerable amount from it. For many of them it is the main area of the practicum in which they feel in charge. One difficulty, however, is that in recent years lack of resources has precluded holding a closing conference, which is so important as an end point and celebration of their research.

In the Teachers College program several projects have significant inquiry elements: the curriculum project, the master's portfolio, the school study, and the child study. We will describe the last two in some detail. The school study is done in the second semester of the full-time year. According to Michele Genor, this study focuses on two questions related to curriculum and community that the students have about their school, for example, how are the students supported in special education services outside my classroom, and what kind of parents get involved at the school? The questions are intended to serve as a framework for understanding the culture of the school and the guiding principles present within that culture. The students attempt to answer the questions by means of observation, document analysis, interviews, and other forms of data collection. They are free to work either individually or with other students placed at their school. Michele said that part of the rationale given to the students for doing the project is that they must learn to be teachers who can "utilize and maximize what their school has to offer. [W]e're very explicit that, when they begin their first year of teaching, they will have to be very resourceful and know how to ask questions and find resources for their students; and in order to have this type of resourcefulness they need to understand the school culture." Goodwin and Lawrence (2002) say of the school study that "it directs students to consider the larger institutional context and its relationship to and influence on what occurs in individual classrooms" (p. 80).

Another major research project in the Teachers College program is a child study, conducted in the first semester of the full-time year. Michele Genor noted that for many students this is their first research project, and accordingly, extensive guidance on data collection is given in the CORE course, along with feedback as the inquiry proceeds. In a journal article, Lin Goodwin (2002) provides details on the child study:

> Students choose one child to follow closely and, over the course of a semester, observe, document, and gather data (including work samples) about this child as a learner and as a community member. Students . . . are free to focus on any child whom they feel they would like to come to know. The reason for this, we tell students, is that any child will benefit from close observation. . . .

The assignment requires a minimum of 6 data collection episodes or observations [now increased to 10], and specifically asks that students observe the
child's engagement with all curriculum areas, the child's life in and out of the
classroom (i.e., on the playground, lunchroom, etc., not home life), and the
child's social life as a member of a classroom community. The emphasis of the
case is coming to know one child well. . . . The case [also] becomes a documentation of the students' own development as teachers, as they puzzle
through questions of practice and learn to critically analyze their own experiences. (p. 139)

In carrying out the study, students are supported by the structure of the
assignment and by interaction with faculty and peers. To begin, students document "any interaction they have witnessed in their daily lives," as a basis for
discussions about objectivity, subjectivity, interpretation, assumptions, and
evidence. The purpose of this activity is to help them see "how easily teachers
can come to hasty conclusions about children" (p. 139). Then, early in the
study, students carry out specific kinds of observations, such as writing an
anecdotal record in which they keep separate "the description, feeling, and
inference sections" (p. 139). As the study progresses, more freedom is permitted, for example, in the data collection techniques used. During the semester,
two smaller segments of the study are submitted to faculty for review before
the final written case is submitted. In responding to these submissions, faculty
"challenge the assumptions students seem to be making about the child" (p.
140). Students write "analytic memos" as they try to interpret the emerging
data, and "a reflective and analytical paper where they compare themselves
with the child they are studying." They conclude the write-up with a statement of instructional implications. Finally, they "present their completed cases
to peers for review and discussion" (p. 140).

On the basis of formal research on this child study assignment, Goodwin
(2002) concluded that students learn a great deal from it. They "are challenged
to rethink what they thought they knew and to consider multiple alternatives"
(p. 140). They come to see that "teaching is always a cross-cultural encounter"
(p. 140). Their entry beliefs about children are significantly altered and deepened. Some who start out seeing their child as "troubled" or "not compre-
hending anything" find that he or she has considerable insights and abilities;
as a result, "they stop blaming children for their failures and start examining
what they need to do to make learning happen" (p. 148). Some who begin
with a simplistic view of teaching acquire "deeper understandings of the reci-
procal and contextual nature of the teaching/learning process" (p. 149). Of 6
students interviewed about the assignment, all became aware of "how inaccu-
rate their initial impressions were" and came to see that "there is no 'general'
child" (p. 152).

Speaking generally of the school and child studies at Teachers College,
Goodwin and Lawrence (2002) comment:

Both studies are designed to engage students in critical examination of teaching and learning and the purpose of schooling. . . . [T]hese assignments render concrete the complexity of teaching and schooling and underscore the myriad decisions that teachers must make in order to teach well. (p. 80)

This statement captures well the central purpose of the student research projects in all three programs we have been describing.

CHALLENGES TO AN INQUIRY APPROACH

In pursuing an inquiry approach in their respective programs, the teacher educators we interviewed reported facing a number of difficulties. These included a shortage of suitable staff, a heavy workload, inadequate resources, and lack of appreciation of the approach among colleagues and even, to a degree, among student teachers. Despite these challenges, however, the interviewees made remarkable statements to the effect that they "would not do it any other way."

Shortage of suitable staff. At the University of Sydney, David Smith noted that spending cuts in recent years had required the use of some faculty who were not suited to an inquiry-based program. This contrasted with the first few years of the MTeach when all those teaching in it "were not only committed to it, but were aware of the principles underpinning it." David elaborated on the kind of faculty needed. Since the students are older and come from all walks of life, they "are incredibly stimulating, but also incredibly challenging; they are not prepared for you to take on the role that you normally might as an instructor in a university." The team attempts to screen new faculty appointed to the program, and they team teach with new faculty and provide them with extensive inservicing; nevertheless, some faculty are unable to make the adjustment.

At OISE/UT we also find that some tenure-track faculty are not able or inclined to adopt an inquiry approach in their preservice teaching. While in a sense they believe in it, the reward structure of the university makes it difficult to for them to spend the time needed, and some do not have enough background in schooling to tackle issues in a way that relates theory to practice. Accordingly, they tend to come into the program, present their ideas in fairly abstract terms, and move out again; and this models a transmission rather than an inquiry approach. It also leaves unaddressed the problem of students lacking support in the practicum and so being afraid to develop constructivist pedagogy. Further, it means there are not enough faculty available to interact with mentor teachers and encourage them toward an inquiry approach. Because of the shortage of tenure-track faculty, we use a large proportion of full-time contract faculty on loan from school boards. These usually make excellent preservice educators, especially when integrated into a faculty team with a clear philosophy and a well-developed program. However, they often lack the background needed to give students a thorough grounding in teacher research.

Inadequate resources. We saw how, at the University of Sydney, financial cutbacks for preservice education have impacted negatively on staffing for the MTeach. In the Mid-Town program, there is insufficient provision for the work of building community, integrating the program around an inquiry focus, visiting schools, and inservicing and recognizing mentor teachers. Of particular concern for the action research is lack of funding for bringing mentor teachers together to study teacher research and giving them release time to attend a final action research conference. For the first two years of the action research projects in Mid-Town a teachers union provided funding for a closing conference, and this had a powerful impact on the whole process. It gave the students something to aim toward and a way of getting feedback on their research and celebrating their achievement. It also meant that the many mentor teachers who attended the conference were able to gain a better understanding of action research, thus placing them in a stronger position to support the research of student teachers in the future.

Lack of appreciation of an inquiry approach. David Smith at the University of Sydney noted that, typically, initiating students into a broad approach to curriculum that is problem-based, inquiry-oriented, and socially aware is not valued as highly by the university as subject-specific instruction: "it has been a battle to get general curriculum onto the agenda and work with it." At OISE/UT, as mentioned, there is inadequate recognition of and support for an inquiry approach on the part of the school of education; in addition, many of the students do not fully appreciate the approach, sometimes wondering whether it will serve them well in the "real world" of teaching. At Teachers College, Anne Sabatini observed that while the situation has improved greatly in recent years, "teacher education is not an easy thing to get up there to the administration," and the workload for preservice faculty is still exceptionally heavy. Michele Genor said that the student teachers, having nothing to compare the program with, often do not see fully what they are learning from it and how valuable it is. Nevertheless, she added, "at the end of the year I remind myself that it's worth it, as I see what happens to them; and also graduates come back and are able to articulate the impact this inquiry focus has had on their emerging practices."

Heavy workload. The heavy workload in preservice education is legendary. This problem is exacerbated by an inquiry approach, which requires extensive community building, integrated planning, considerable individual student support, and working closely with schools and mentor teachers. Michele Genor at Teachers College commented that there is often an assumption at

the university that those who teach late afternoons and evenings are free during the day to attend meetings and so forth, whereas in fact those involved in
teacher education often spend much of their day in schools. The extensive
underlying work required by an inquiry approach does not fit easily into the
categories of scholarship, service, and so on, and so tends to go unrecognized.
A comment by Anne Sabatini at Teachers College provides a fitting conclusion to this section and the chapter. Like Michele, Anne noted the challenges
but also reiterated the importance of employing such an approach in preservice education:

> Preservice is extraordinarily time consuming, and sometimes I wonder why
> I'm in it because I could just be teaching courses that have nothing to do
> with anything except me and the students and the course content. There's a
> lot of cooperation and collaboration and sharing of tasks . . . a lot of time for
> discussion. . . . [But] I feel that in preparing teachers for today's schools, it
> has to be this kind of model. . . . I wouldn't choose to do it any other way . . .
> they have to see the bigger picture and understand what it means to be a
> community.

CHAPTER 4

Building Community in the Program

Obviously we talk about it all the time, how great the social events are, and how everyone gets on. But moving that into teaching, that sets the foundation that this is a social profession. You're not teaching by yourself to some kids in isolation, you are there with all these other people. . . . [And in the practicum] you are working with the other student teachers going through the same experiences, and sharing things with them, learning from them, getting different perspectives on things, getting different ideas.

—Paul, OISE/UT Mid-Town preservice student

Constructivism today has a strong sociocultural emphasis. As discussed in chapter 1, constructivist educators are now more aware of how learning is influenced by the larger society in which we live and by our teachers and peers. The influence occurs both through unconscious absorption of ideas and practices from those around us and consciously as we dialogue with others. Communal learning is often positive because of the insights we gain from others, but it can be negative as we are indoctrinated into problematic outlooks.

Student teachers are no exception to this phenomenon. Accordingly, it is important to ensure as far as possible that the community experience of a preservice program is strong and has a positive impact. A supportive community can provide a context for critiquing societal practices and negotiating ideas about teaching and learning. As Linda Kroll at Mills College said in her interview:

If you're going to talk about issues of social justice, equity, and excellence and have hard conversations about things like race and discrimination and how you feel about those things, then you have to have a safe place to talk about it. And if you are going to take risks, showing that you don't know something, there has to be a safe place. So . . . the first thing you have to do is establish a community in your classroom where people feel free to say what they think and where it's okay to make mistakes.

Such a setting also serves as a model of community-based education, allowing students to see firsthand how valuable this approach can be and how to establish it in their own classrooms. Further, when the community extends into the practicum, it gives student teachers the support they need to develop constructivist pedagogy in a school climate that often discourages such an approach.

Is it appropriate from a constructivist point of view to impose a certain type of program on preservice students, namely, a community-oriented one? Is this not itself indoctrinative? Given student teachers' extensive past experience of individualistic, cognitively oriented education (Lortie, 1975), we believe it is legitimate to expose them systematically to a more communal approach. However, it is essential that they have constant opportunities to disagree and propose alternatives. The particular kind of classroom community we have in mind may not be feasible, or it may not suit everyone. Constructivism requires that we work *with* student teachers in exploring the type of community they need in both preservice and school contexts.

COMMUNITY AND LEARNING

We wish to stress at the outset that, on a social constructivist view, community is not just a frill: it is fundamental to effective learning. As Dewey said: "We never educate directly, but indirectly by means of the environment" (Dewey, 1916, p. 32); and "education is essentially a social process. This quality is realized in the degree in which individuals form a community group" (Dewey, 1938, p. 58). Even if students wished to, they could not live in their own bubble while in the classroom. The class milieu continually impinges on their thoughts, emotions, and relationships; it interprets the messages they receive from the teacher and other sources. It also provides them with constant sociocultural experiences.

Especially important for knowledge construction are the ideas students receive from their peers. Unfortunately, student teachers often see community merely in affective terms, as an enjoyable concomitant to their learning. They look to experts, not each other, for answers to their pedagogical questions: cover the material quickly and let us go early, they sometimes say. They do not realize that the "expert" ideas in books and journal articles are quite abstract as they stand, and so have little practical value. Only as the ideas are interpreted and given concrete form do they become useful; and in this process, the countless qualifications, suggestions, and stories offered by peers are invaluable, arising as they do from a wide array of perspectives and experiences. Of course, communal learning varies greatly in its effectiveness, and this can be a source of frustration to students. However, we should not therefore pursue noncommunal learning, which is not an option; rather we should work to ensure that the wealth of insights the students have among them, along with those of the instructors, are brought to bear in a very effective manner on the issues at hand.

In previous research on our own program, we have found that a close preservice community has a strong impact on learning (Beck & Kosnik, 2001, pp. 942–46; Kosnik & Beck, 2003, pp. 108–109). Several of the "softer" effects of a community emphasis are perhaps to be expected: group loyalty, willingness to pitch in, caring for one another, inclusiveness, even personal and social growth. What surprised us was the extent of the impact in more academic and technical areas. These included:

- high level of participation in whole class and small group discussions and activities
- high quality of discussion and group work, notably in connection with the action research projects
- growth in awareness of the value of collaboration and ability and willingness to engage in it; specifically, willingness to seek help and resources from fellow student teachers
- willingness to take risks in practicum settings and implement fundamental changes in approach to teaching
- willingness to express their point of view and question each other's and faculty opinions (while maintaining positive relationships)
- inclination and ability to foster community and collaboration in their own classrooms

On the whole, we were more aware of these effects than the students. However, when interviewed, some students showed considerable knowledge of what they were learning as a result of the community experience. For example, Jennifer early in the year commented: "We are bonding as a class and learning." Then halfway through the year she said: "I will really miss the people, just the special development of being part of a group. . . . A lot of the things we've been introduced to . . . have helped us reflect in certain ways which, when shared together as a group, can provide expansion for all of us." And Janet, a science graduate planning to teach at the primary/junior level, observed:

> Teaching science is very tricky. . . . Which is where this networking thing is going to come in. I just see some amazing stuff come out of people in our program. It's just brilliant stuff, and if they can do it and I can get to know them then I can do it.

As Peterson (1992) says: "When community exists, learning is strengthened—everyone is smarter, more ambitious, and productive." It is the connection between community experience and academic and professional learning that provides much of the rationale for community building in preservice programs and other educational settings.

THREE EXAMPLES OF COMMUNITY-BASED PROGRAMS

In discussing the nature of a community-based preservice program and how one can be established, we will again give illustrations from three programs we view as social constructivist. As in previous chapters, we will draw mainly on interviews with faculty in the programs but also on published reports and other documents. The programs highlighted in this chapter are ones that pay particular attention to community; however, we wish to emphasize that they have many qualities in addition to their community orientation. Like the other programs described in the book, they also stress integration, inquiry, and equity to a high degree. We begin with a brief introduction to the three programs.

Edith Cowan University's Middle Years Graduate Diploma

The Graduate Diploma in Education (Middle Years of Schooling) at Edith Cowan University in Perth, Western Australia was planned from the outset as a cohort program with a strong community orientation. It is a 10-month post-baccalaureate program with an enrollment of approximately 80 students. Apart from community, its emphases include constructivism, integration of theory and practice, and a "middle school" philosophy, by which is meant (among other things) integrating subject areas and being adolescent-centered rather than subject-centered. There are 4 main faculty on the program team, all of whom volunteered to teach in the program and are committed to its philosophy. Lesley Newhouse-Maiden commented:

> For 6 years I was involved in a secondary program . . . where we were encouraging the student teachers to move from their subject orientation and actually work together on an integrated program and then evaluate it, adopting a middle school philosophy. . . . So when this [middle school] proposal came forward, I just jumped at it. I thought this is just wonderful, it is something I've always wanted to do.

Community building in the program is facilitated by having the cohort do their courses together under the direction of the faculty team. There are just 8 courses (plus 2 practicum courses), which are taken by all students. Further, the courses are integrated through an underlying philosophy of middle schooling, extensive use of group discussion and collaborative activities in teaching the courses, and a special module called Integrated Studies. Beyond the classroom, community is fostered through an orientation program in the first week, a daily tea time, other social events, clustering students during the practicum, and an online communication platform.

Mills College's Preservice Master of Arts in Education

The preservice M.A. at Mills College in Oakland, California has an enrollment of 60 students in its 10-month "credential program," which qualifies them to teach at either the elementary or secondary level. After gaining their credential, most students continue to study full- or part-time for up to 4 years to complete the M.A. Our focus here is mainly on the 10-month credential program, which is done full-time and involves intensive field experience. The students are in practicum placements throughout the program, going to their school 4 or 5 mornings a week. Some students spend 1 afternoon a week as well at their school site. Campus classes are held in the afternoon.

The cohort and faculty team structure of the credential program was chosen in part to facilitate community. Linda Kroll, a co-director of the program, explained that the program's view is that "teaching is about relationships." The year begins with orientation activities in which students learn about each other, the faculty, and the goals of the program. The whole cohort is together for certain main courses given by senior faculty; for other courses and the practicum there are smaller groupings, thus enabling students to get to know each other in greater depth. Emphasis is placed on students working together and presenting to each other. Anna Richert, another co-director of the program, commented: "[O]ur students care about each other, which is something we value deeply."

OISE/UT's Mid-Town Bachelor of Education

Our own program, the Mid-Town B.Ed. cohort program at OISE/University of Toronto, was described in part in the previous chapter when discussing an inquiry emphasis in preservice education. Here we focus especially on its community orientation, which has been central to the program since its inception in 1989. For most of the first decade we were school-based; this helped in establishing a tradition of close community because for 4 days a week we were physically together off-campus. The program is small (just 65 students), has a faculty team, and has many core courses that we integrate as much as possible. Efforts to build community include orientation activities, a 2-day retreat early in the year, getting-to-know-you activities in class, social events, and clustering of students in partner schools during the practicum.

The community dimension is stressed in the program's vision statement, which lists the goal of establishing "a supportive learning community in which diversity is accepted, personal expression is encouraged, and everyone feels they can make a contribution." Graduates and current students often refer to their experience of community as the single most important aspect of the program, and this is how we have come to view it ourselves. As outlined in the previous section, apart from direct social and emotional benefits we have found that a close community aids attainment of many other program goals as well.

We turn now to a thematic discussion of community-based preservice programming and how to implement it, providing examples from the three programs. We wish to stress, however, that while these programs have been very successful in establishing such an approach, the process involved is not always easy or straightforward. In a concluding section we will review some of the challenges encountered even in these programs.

CONDITIONS FOR COMMUNITY

Although community can be achieved to a degree in virtually any preservice program, certain conditions facilitate community formation. These include having a relatively small cohort, a team of faculty assigned specifically to the program, and suitable space for campus classes. We begin by briefly discussing each of these conditions.

Small size. Having a small cohort makes community development more feasible since it allows for closer relationships among students and between faculty and students. Opinions vary regarding the optimal size of a cohort, but the number favored tends to range from about 25 to 80. In the credential program at Mills College a cohort of 60 is seen as allowing for financial viability on the one hand and close community on the other. However, for many purposes the main cohort is divided into smaller groups such as subject-area classes, practicum seminar groups, and practicum clusters in schools.

At Edith Cowan University, 80 students are enrolled in the middle school program, but again subgrouping occurs both on campus and in the schools. According to Lesley Newhouse-Maiden, "80 is a good size. You can actually get to know every student and their needs . . . [and] it gives us a bigger faculty team." At OISE/UT, the 600 elementary B.Ed. student teachers are divided into nine cohorts, of which Mid-Town is one. The 65 students in Mid-Town are in turn split into 2 groups for most classes and into yet smaller groups for the practicum. In the early years of the program we had a cohort of 30; however, we came to the view (as at Edith Cowan) that a larger cohort is preferable because it allows for a bigger faculty team. Also, in a larger group students are exposed to a wider diversity of viewpoints and have greater opportunity to find kindred spirits.

A faculty team. Having a faculty team (including contract faculty) assigned to a program is another key factor in community development. Not all team members need be full-time in the program, so long as they are committed to the cohort and have time to participate in it. With a faculty team greater program coherence can be achieved, community building can be coordinated, and students can identify with a group of instructors. A further advantage is that the faculty can model community and collaboration rather than just talking about it. This is important, both to show students that we really believe in the approach and to give them concrete examples of how to implement it.

At Mills College most of the faculty in the credential program are tenure-track, but the contract faculty are also full team members. The whole team meets at least monthly, and there are other regular meetings of faculty concerned with particular dimensions of the program. All the faculty we interviewed (one of whom was on contract) spoke of the team in glowing terms. For example, Linda Kroll commented: "[T]his is the most collaborative and collegial faculty I have ever experienced." And Phil Tucher said:

> [What I appreciate here] is being part of a collaboration of adults . . . [being able to] surround myself with people who care deeply about their students . . . and come together at least monthly to dig into shared issues, that's what was so attractive to me. . . . I want other people to value the work I do and the learning I have to go through, and see this as a shared endeavor, because it is way too hard for any of us to do alone.

The middle years program at Edith Cowan University has a director (currently Terry DeJong); however, most decisions are made by the team. Rod Chadbourne, founding director of the program, stated that "there are very few executive decisions, any major decisions are brought to the committee." This was echoed by Terry, who said:

> [T]he way we go about planning is very collaborative. We are responsible individually for putting our own course together, including the lectures and workshops. But invariably when we sit down and talk about the process we come up with new ideas. . . . The thing I enjoy most is that it gives me a good picture of the middle years program as a whole. When I worked at the University of X, I did my little bit, and although I did talk with colleagues it was very much a segregated approach; and that was never very satisfactory.

Bill Leadbetter noted that "across the spectrum of courses, we practice a variety of pedagogical styles. In Mathematics we form 3 classes, each with a different instructor; in Science & Environment we include drama, song, and student performance; and English is taught in a more traditional manner. In one way or another, we can all get involved in nearly all the courses." Rod Chadbourne observed: "The team approach deprivatizes the courses; what we learn from each other we can teach to the students."

Suitable space. Space is very important for community. The whole cohort should be able to come together in familiar surroundings, with facilities for dividing into class sections and small groups. When the Mid-Town program was housed in a school we had our own rooms that were not used for any other purpose. Now that we are at the university we have regular use of a large classroom that accommodates everyone, with a smaller room and breakout areas nearby. From year to year we have to protect this arrangement, as the staff concerned with allocating space in the university can easily forget our unusual needs. At Mills College, the credential program benefits from the fact that the Department of Education is relatively small and has its own attractive and compact building. There are suitable spaces for large and small classes and group work, and the offices of core faculty are easily accessible.

At Edith Cowan, space in the recently built school of education building was carefully designed for the middle school program, with flexible facilities and movable furniture that allow the cohort either to meet together or divide into subgroups. Rod Chadbourne reported: "We were involved in planning the new building, and we designed our space so we can open up the rooms and all get in the one area. For a 3-hour class, we can have all 80 students in 1 group or split them into 3 groups, each in a different room." Given the emphasis on teas, the kitchen facilities were a matter of interest. Rod said:

> We insisted on having a kitchen in the new building, where the students could have their teatime. Some people opposed that, asking why they should have these facilities; and we said well, you know, during that half hour after their class, we want them to have social interaction and also share professional things, for example, what's happening out in the schools.

A CORE PROGRAM

The conditions described above are very important, but they do not by themselves guarantee the emergence of a close and supportive community. Goodlad (1990b) found that even small preservice programs often lack a sense of community; and at OISE/UT we have observed that the community experience varies from one cohort to another, even though all have roughly the same number of students. Indeed, if not well-handled, a cohort structure can help reinforce conservative attitudes as student teachers, in their anxiety about the "realities" of schooling, band together to resist constructivist approaches (Howey, 1996; Tom, 1997). However favorable the conditions, deliberate steps must be taken to foster community.

Developing a largely common, integrated program supports community formation by giving student teachers a shared experience, helping them get to know one another, and allowing them to explore ideas together in a social constructivist manner. Goodlad (1990b) talks of the lack of community in preservice programs where the student body changes from one class to another. Bullough and Gitlin (1995) describe the advantages of a situation where a cohort of students can revisit the same key issues again and again during the program.

In the Mid-Town program at OISE/UT, apart from one elective education course and another teaching-subject course for junior/intermediate candidates, the whole cohort takes the same set of courses: Curriculum & Instruction (including language/literacy, math, science, phys ed, the arts, and action research), Teacher Education Seminar (including program planning, teacher research, special education, and school law), Psychology, and School & Society. Further, the team works hard to integrate these courses through joint planning, integrated coverage of key topics, team teaching and assessment, use of common or similar evaluation rubrics, and adherence to a common pedagogical approach (as outlined in the vision statement).

In the Edith Cowan middle school program, as noted, all students take the same 8 courses (plus the practicum): 4 pedagogy courses (Science, Math, English, and Science & Environment) and 4 foundations courses (Adolescent Development, Curriculum & Pedagogy, Context & Philosophy, and Alienation to Engagement). There are no electives. According to Rod Chadbourne, "[we] just don't have time in a 1-year program [to have electives]." Additional topics are covered in the Wednesday Forum and in special workshops: for example, Teachers and the Law, Inclusive Education, Special Education, Teaching English to Foreign Students, Boys and Education, and Behavior Management; and there are sessions on Music, Art, and Drama. However, once again, the whole cohort engages in these activities together, with a combination of whole group and subgroup classes and small group work.

Apart from having a common set of courses and other activities at Edith Cowan, much is done to integrate the various components of the campus program with each other and with the practicum (which is distributed across the year). Rod Chadbourne commented that, "at a philosophical level, the program components are integrated not only by the focus on a single developmental stage (early adolescence), that is, a commitment to making middle years education adolescent-centered, but also by a commitment to constructivism, community, and the integration of theory and practice." Rod spoke of the flexibility permitted by the university to modify content, hours, and requirements of courses so interconnections are possible. He noted the benefits of the resulting integration:

> [With] this program, more than any other preservice teaching I've done, I've enjoyed a sense of knowing what I'm doing, seeing where it fits into the whole program. Before, I taught 1 out of maybe 30 courses, and I tried to do a good job and got satisfaction from it, but I didn't know where it fitted into the totality of the program. With this program, because it is just 1 year, and we're involved in teaching across several courses and meeting as a program committee . . . I have a great sense of how it fits together. And that's quite a responsibility, because at the end of the day we are virtually giving our graduates a licence to practice, a licence to teach, and we are held accountable for doing so; but the upside is that it's nice to have a strong sense of the exit outcomes of our students and have our work guided by that.

In the Mills College credential program, integration across courses is achieved by constant reference to the "six principles" of the program. These may be summarized as: (i) teaching as a moral, caring act; (ii) collegiality; (iii) reflection and inquiry; (iv) teaching as a political act; (v) learning as contructivist and developmental; and (vi) acquisition of both subject matter and professional knowledge. All 4 interviewees at Mills spoke of the effectiveness of these principles in pulling the program together. For example, Linda Kroll

said: "[Having] principles unifies the program . . . as a result of those principles and beliefs, we build all kinds of bridges within the credential program . . .
we're really all on the same path." And Phil Tucher commented:

> [The program] being principle-based . . . has brought incredible coher-
> ence. . . . [B]eing in a new job . . . the learning curve is very steep, but being
> grounded in the idea that my job is . . . to understand deeply what those six
> principles are for us and . . . have my students understand those principles
> when they leave here, has brought incredible clarity of purpose.

Beyond the principles, other mechanisms are used to integrate the Mills
credential program. There are frequent planning meetings of the whole faculty team and subgroups within it. Anna Richert remarked that "we spend a
lot of time . . . talking about different activities, things we're doing in our
classes." And Dave Donahue reported:

> I'm very aware of what student teachers do in the Curriculum & Instruction
> class; so in the Reading & Writing class, if I ask them to develop a lesson
> plan that incorporates explicit instruction, I'll make it due after they have
> already done lesson planning in Curriculum & Instruction, so they can use
> the same lesson plan or build on that. Or I will sometimes choose readings
> knowing they have read them in other classes. . . . So the courses are discrete
> but not totally fragmented. . . . [And] there are some assignments that they
> can hand in for several different people. For example, one of the assignments
> at the end of the year is a unit of instruction, and ideally they will have
> already handed in pieces of that to several people. And the final project they
> submit is a portfolio of their teaching that incorporates most of the work
> they've done for all the different courses. . . . And within the [total] cohort
> they share it all; we spend a whole day where, rather than just walking us
> through the portfolio, they talk about what they have learned in the process
> of putting it together, and who they are as teachers, and who they've become.
> It's partly presenting and partly celebrating.

VARIED SUBGROUPINGS

In all the cohort programs we are aware of, community is fostered both in the
total cohort and in subgroups. Students need to relate to the whole cohort so
that they are exposed to a wider range of backgrounds, ideas, and personalities; but subgroups facilitate deeper sharing and stronger support (which in
turn strengthen the whole community). A further advantage of having the two
levels is that being in a larger group helps student teachers understand the
dynamics within typical school classes, while being in a smaller group affords
an experience similar to that with teacher colleagues.

In the Mid-Town program, apart from moving between the whole cohort
and subgroups, we have found it important to vary the composition of the

subgroups as much as possible. This allows for greater variety of experience and helps avoid the development of cliques within the cohort. For example, while we usually split the cohort in half for classes, we often mix primary/junior and junior/intermediate student teachers in the two halves, calling them simply "Groups 1 and 2." This ensures that the typically more child-centered primary/junior students mingle with the usually more subject-oriented junior/intermediate students.

In the Mills College program, too, attention is given to forging links between different categories of students within the cohort. Here the processes are more complex because of the diversity of streams involved. Linda Kroll reported:

> The first activity [at the retreat] is getting together in smaller cohort groups. . . . We want our students to see themselves as teachers first and specialists second, so we form these cohorts of about 10 students each, with members from each of the program strands.

Similarly, Anna Richert described what she does in her cohort-wide course: "I put them in different groups across grade levels and subject areas and have them discuss why it is important for, say, a third-grade teacher to talk to a high school physics teacher, what it is they have in common. And we really problematize those positions."

At Edith Cowan, Rod Chadbourne described the transitions made between whole cohort, medium range, and small group activities:

> So we might have a 1-hour session with the whole cohort, and then a 2-hour workshop where the students are split into 3 groups of 25 to 30, equivalent to what is out there in school classrooms. . . . Even during the whole cohort session, students sit at tables of 5 or 6 and there is some small group work in the table groupings, in addition to whole cohort lectures and discussion. In the workshops of 25 to 30, similarly, there is both whole group and small group work. Overall, during a 3-hour session I would say about 25 percent of time is spent in whole cohort activities and 75 percent in small group or workshop-type activities.

Sometimes when the whole cohort is together they are with one faculty member, and at other times there is a team-teaching situation. According to Terry DeJong, the Cowan team emphasizes not only varying the size of the groups but also "giving students a good mix of experiences within the [class] community."

> [W]e have devised the groups to maximize the mix of gender and also the faculty that students interact with. So, for example, no student should have me as a workshop facilitator more than once or twice, depending on how many workshops I'm involved in; and students by the end of the program should have been in workshops where they have come to know every single professor. And that takes a bit of engineering . . . much of the time we don't give them a choice about which groups they are in.

EXPLICIT DISCUSSION OF COMMUNITY

Another key strategy in community building is to discuss the value of community in education, both in classes and informally as the opportunity arises. This of course is an important part of explaining to the students the nature of a social constructivist approach. The discussion should address both the school setting and preservice education itself. The students' own experiences should be part of the focus: their memories of schooling, how they are feeling about the preservice community, and their current experiences in practicum placements.

In our interviews, several faculty stressed the importance of talking about community with student teachers. For example, Anna Richert at Mills College noted the concern that secondary candidates, because of their past academic attainments, might be "very competitive with one another" and so undermine community in the cohort. Accordingly, when working with the secondary students she addresses explicitly the need for community. She makes the point that "We're in this together," and poses such questions as "What is your responsibility to one another in this community?" and "How do we work together?" At Edith Cowan, Rod Chadbourne commented:

> Of all the programs I've taught in over my 33 years [of preservice teaching], this has the greatest sense of community. And I think one reason is that we've identified that as an integral part of the program, we've put it in writing in the student handouts, and we've included it in our lectures: we discuss the theory of community, saying this is the rationale for it, this is why it's worth spending time on, and these are the things you can do. . . . [And as] an explicit part of our program . . . I literally outline the different levels of teacher-collegial relations: for example, sharing stories of teaching; sharing resources; joint planning; [and] doing joint projects, working together to decide what you're going to do and how you're going to do it.

COLLABORATIVE LEARNING ACTIVITIES

Often when authors write about "class community" or "learning communities" in education their focus is on collaborative *learning*; that is, the emphasis is largely academic. Here, in line with social constructivist theory, we have taken a more holistic approach to community; we advocate a strongly social and emotional experience that we believe is essential for depth of understanding. Nevertheless, collaborative learning is an important component in constructivist teaching and teacher education. An interactive relationship exists between collaboration and community. On the one hand, collaboration is dependent on community: unless students know each other and get on well together, the effectiveness of their collaboration will be limited. But equally, collaborative activity strengthens community, since it ensures that students get to know each other better and also helps them develop social inclinations and skills.

As noted previously, both the Edith Cowan and Mills College programs use collaborative group work extensively. According to Rod Chadbourne at Cowan, "joint tasks" are probably the most important means of promoting collegiality and community among teachers. And Anna Richert at Mills gave an example of how she implements collaboration in her cohort-wide course:

> I talk about curriculum as the "technology" of teachers' work, so that students get a sense that . . . creating it, thinking about it, implementing it, and assessing it are core aspects of what teachers do and need to do together. I put them into groups, with one elementary, one middle school, and one high school teacher. I assign each group a concept, such as "cycles," "cause and effect," or "hypothesis and proof," and they have to talk about why this is a foundational idea in the discipline they choose. . . . Then we have a poster conference, and they have to defend their concept in terms of how foundational it is to the discipline they're teaching and how it has transformative potential in the life of the child.

In the Mid-Town program a high proportion of the learning activities and assignments involve working in pairs or small groups. However, we find the students vary in their appreciation of this approach. They certainly enjoy it, but sometimes they feel they are not learning enough. This suggests to us on the one hand that we need to develop more activities that are not only interactive and enjoyable but also very effective in promoting learning; and on the other hand that we need to find better ways to help students see how much they are in fact learning through the collaborative work.

ORIENTATION EVENTS

It is important to set a community tone right from the beginning of the program, before students settle into an individualistic pattern in line with their past educational experiences. The middle school faculty team at Edith Cowan takes the opportunity provided by the university's general orientation week to discuss the purpose of community with the cohort and begin to build community through group activities. At Mills College, Linda Kroll described their orientation retreat:

> The first event for all our credential folks each year is a 1-day retreat. We go off campus to Marin Headlands, a very beautiful place about 45 minutes from the campus, and we do serious but fun activities. The first activity is getting together in smaller cohort groups . . . from each of the program strands, and we focus on the six program principles. There are 6 groups, and each student is given a little piece of paper with a quote that exemplifies their group's principle, and they have to find their group and then figure out what

the principle is. . . . And we have them do some readings [on issues of diversity and equity] before they come and launch a discussion of those readings which will continue throughout the year. Also, we have them bring a cultural artifact about themselves to share in their cohort. And there are a number of other things we do during the day, and it's to get to know each other and reflect on: What are we about? Where are we going in this program? What's our goal for the next 10 months?

In the Mid-Town program at OISE/UT, the first cohort meeting during registration week involves a minimum of administrative information and a maximum of community building. Various activities are used to help the student teachers relax, learn about each other and the faculty, and understand the concept of a community-oriented class. In one activity, for example, prizes are given out for people who have come the longest distance to attend the program, have been to the most exotic places, have had the most interesting jobs, have met the most famous people, have the largest number of siblings, have the youngest parent, and so on. This leads to much laughter and considerable sharing about themselves; it also establishes a certain approach to the program community. Looking back over the year, one of the Mid-Town students commented:

> Right from the very get-go, we came into the room [on registration day] on a really stressful day, and all of a sudden it was like this oasis: Hi everybody, welcome, EF is going to do a reading, and now we're going to introduce the faculty. We're going to have a great time, dah, dah, dah, a math card trick from GH, and oh let's all meet each other. It was so not stressful; it was everything the opposite of what we had just gone through. So it really set the tone for the rest of the year.

At the end of the meeting we distribute the Mid-Town Handbook and give a "homework" assignment, namely, to read the Handbook and come to the first class with 3 questions about the program. This sets the stage for learning about the program but the focus has been on community, which is perhaps the key "message" we want them to take from this first session.

The main Mid-Town orientation activity is a 2-day retreat held in the third or fourth week of the program. The retreat center is a short distance from Toronto, set in a lovely park beside a river. After an initial social time and settling in, we have a workshop on "learning styles" in which students and faculty learn a considerable amount about themselves and each other. After lunch comes perhaps the highlight of the retreat: the students' sharing of their All About Me books, prepared as a language arts activity in the weeks prior to the retreat. The sharing is done in two ways: in small groups initially, and then by laying the books on tables for people to peruse during the rest of the retreat. The students go to great lengths to make the books enjoyable and informative, including excerpts from their diaries, photographs, computer generated art work, report cards from elementary school, wedding invitations, and so on. As they read the books they learn about their fellow classmates, see many examples of bookmaking, and experience firsthand elements of an effective language arts program. Later in the day there are outdoor activities, such as ultimate frisbee, touch football, hiking down to the river, or simply sitting on the patio soaking up the sunshine. In an early evening session, recent Mid-Town graduates come to meet with the new students in groups and discuss some of the challenges of the preservice program and of being a beginning teacher. This is followed by a party that continues into the night. The next morning, a facilitator from a school board conducts a highly interactive workshop designed to help students and faculty get to know one another further, acquire community building techniques, and understand more fully the importance of community in educational settings. During the closing ceremony, each student or faculty member makes a short speech about another person (whose name they drew from a hat the previous day) and what they learned about them during the retreat.

OTHER COMMUNITY BUILDING STRATEGIES

Beyond the orientation phase, there should be other community building efforts over the course of the program, both in and out of class. Even where these are not initiated by the faculty team, students should be aware that the team supports them and sees them as fundamental to the program rather than just an extra. After so many years of often impersonal and individualistic education, students need strong encouragement to go in this direction.

Social and getting-to-know-you activities. In the Edith Cowan program, as we have noted, there are the morning and afternoon teas. When we interviewed the Cowan faculty we asked innocently whether the teas are every week or every two weeks, and were told they are every day, sometimes twice a day! Rod Chadbourne spoke about these:

> We initiated the idea of the tea social club at the beginning of the year, but the students run it themselves. They collect the money, buy the tea and biscuits, and do all the work; we have a half-hour teatime once a day, sometimes twice a day. There is a kitchen and a balcony upstairs, and there is a really nice sense of spaciousness, moving from the kitchen through to the balcony. . . . They've also organized a lunch for next week [fourth week into the year] to which everyone is invited. And for the last 2 weeks they have been debating among themselves how they can start a social group, a sport group, and things like going to pubs together.

The Cowan faculty also spoke of getting-to-know-you activities in class. Terry DeJong reported: "We've insisted on them wearing name labels. We're now in the third or fourth week, so people are probably starting to get a bit lax about it, but we were very insistent and kept on coming back and saying 'We need to get to know you, and you need to get to know each other'." Rod Chadbourne said: "[W]e try in our sessions with them to disclose a fair bit about ourselves, without overdoing it . . . and we encourage them to do the same, even to the point of having a small group activity: 'You've got two minutes to send a telegram about yourself, what would you say?'—that sort of thing."

In the Mid-Town program, as noted before, we place very strong emphasis on the social aspect, with faculty playing a substantial facilitating role. Getting-to-know-you activities continue in class during the year, and at the beginning of many classes there is an "announcements" time when upcoming social events are discussed and students talk about their involvements on campus or elsewhere. Every 3 or 4 weeks, beginning with the first day of the program, a large proportion of the group (including faculty) go to the pub together after class. Several times during the year there is an evening party for the whole cohort in the home of a faculty member or student, and smaller groups get together from time to time for other outings. If a student is competing in a sporting event or performing in a concert, a number of us will attend. At the end of the year a large contingent from Mid-Town attend the graduation formal.

Over the years we have found that faculty and students in Mid-Town vary in the time or inclination they have to join in the social activities, but all attend at least some; and even when only a few are present it has a positive impact on the community. We have been surprised how quickly the students see the implications of the social emphasis for their own teaching. For example, in a year-end interview Anita said:

> I hope I will be in a school situation where the principal and teachers are supportive of this kind of environment. If not, then at least in my classroom I will build a community, you know, a respect for being able to share ideas; they feel comfortable, I feel comfortable too . . . and I'm listening to the kids, the stuff they're talking about, and trying to make that little connection.

Electronic communication. Communication via the internet reinforces the other community building activities. It also provides opportunities for sharing professional information and for becoming familiar with communication technology. The Mid-Town conference at OISE/UT has icons for general messages and specific categories such as curriculum resources, assignments, and social events. The general conference is especially popular; about 7 or 8 messages a day on average are posted, seeking or sharing information with respect to teaching materials, websites, job applications, assignment requirements, program changes, strikes, upcoming events, outings, and more personal matters. A great deal of warmth and humor is evident in these exchanges, with people going to considerable lengths to help individuals and the group as a whole. While some postings come from faculty, the great majority are from students.

Linda Kroll noted that Mills College has a Listserve for each year of the credential program, which includes the student group of 60 and the faculty who are working with them. "These Listserves are formed on Yahoo, so they continue long after the cohort graduates." At Edith Cowan, Rod Chadbourne reported:

> We have a middle years discussion board on the campus homepage, and the students have the opportunity to post messages on anything they need help with or have concerns about. And in fact last year's cohort, who have their own graduates' discussion board, have begun to look at and respond to what some of this year's students are saying; and some of this year's students have posted messages on their board. So there's the beginnings of what could be quite an interesting cross-communication between current students and graduates.

A sense of program identity and history.   Steps should be taken to ensure that the cohort has a sense of identity and continuity. Finding an attractive or informative name for the program is important in this process; and students should be made aware of the program's distinctive philosophy and how it has evolved. In the middle school program at Edith Cowan the faculty team keeps in touch with graduates of the program and connects them to current students. In OISE/UT's Mid-Town program a sense of history is fostered by having graduates come back to talk about such matters as how to get the most out of the program, the action research process, and how to survive the first year of teaching. We also take photographs at special events and share them with the cohort. An activity we have found especially valuable is to have each student at the end of the year write a letter of encouragement and advice to a student in the next cohort; we then share these letters with the new students in the first week of classes.

At Mills College, the program's six principles and overarching focus on equity are discussed with students from the beginning of the year and this helps create a sense of identity. In addition, as the new teachers continue in the M.A. program after the credential year they come together in a group called "MEET." This is made up of graduates from several years, so it is not the original cohort; however, they themselves are a cohort and this provides another opportunity for community building and mutual mentoring. Furthermore, the linking of successive cohorts is aided by use of Mills graduates as mentor teachers and by a program called "Mills Teacher Scholars" that supports graduates in continuing to do research on their practice.

MODELING COMMUNITY

As the saying goes, "We teach who we are." The ideas and attitudes exhibited in our behavior have at least as much impact on students as our formal statements. This is in keeping with the social constructivist emphasis on learning through one's total life experience. Accordingly, if we want preservice students to adopt a community approach to teaching we should model this in the program itself.

Preservice faculty who implement the type of program discussed in this chapter are already modeling community. By opting for this approach they indicate their belief that community is important; and they also help students see "how to do it." However, we wish to mention two further ways to model a community emphasis, namely, by adopting a community approach within the faculty team itself and by showing care and support toward the students.

Community in the faculty team.   Practicing community among the faculty provides a clear example to the students of a communal approach to teaching. At Edith Cowan University Bill Leadbetter noted that, coming from outside teacher education (his background was in history), "I've learned about being a preservice teacher through our working together." He added: "Because we try to model the sort of educational values we want our students to adopt, we have built a very effective team. We work together well, challenge each other well, and care for each other. It is both personal and professional."

In the interviews at Mills College, as noted before, faculty spoke of collaboration among team members. Focusing here more specifically on the sense of community in the team, Dave Donahue said: "I have talked to friends of mine who are faculty members elsewhere, and I'm amazed when they talk about how isolated and alone they feel, including through the whole tenure process; and I've never felt that way here." Later he remarked: "When I entered the department I felt so welcomed. . . . I felt like I was becoming part of a place where we are all in it together." Anna Richert observed:

> This group of 8 people gets along famously. I really do feel a close friendship with the people I work with. . . . [To] a new faculty person coming here we would say . . . let us hear from you what you care about so we can really get to know you, because it's a tight faculty and we want you to become part of our community . . . we don't want you on the margins.

In the Mid-Town program, too, a close relationship develops within the faculty team. This occurs partly through planning and teaching together, as described earlier, but also through many informal conversations, email and phone communications, and socializing together whether by ourselves or at general cohort gatherings. A key feature of the Mid-Town program is the integration of contract and tenure-track faculty on the team. In interviews of contract staff on their experience in the program, Linda reported: "As soon as I was hired I felt part of the community and was invited into the community in a variety of ways . . . everybody seemed very interested in having me around." Elizabeth said: "What I really liked immediately was the idea of community and support. . . . I was happily surprised that it wasn't as isolating as graduate work can be." And Sheila commented:

> We had a faculty team in Mid-Town that worked together and helped pick one another up or helped cover. . . . And people didn't make you feel guilty . . . everybody just kept a really positive attitude. . . . [And in practicum supervision] when a student ended up in difficulty, I was lucky I had a team behind me and I could come back and say, "Okay, Clare, this is what the situation is, how do we resolve this?"

Caring for the student teachers. Another way of modeling community is to support the students both on campus and in their practicum placements. As they see the faculty's care toward them, they come to understand the caring role of the teacher in a class community. In the Edith Cowan middle school program, as we have seen, the faculty plan the campus experience in detail, down to making sure there are suitable rooms and furnishings for classes and facilities for tea. Terry DeJong commented that faculty are responsible for "attending to student needs, including pastoral care." In the field, team members play a substantial role in practicum supervision, the aspect of the program that typically causes preservice students the most anxiety. Lesley Newhouse-Maiden reported that faculty not only provide support to individual students but also liaise with the partner schools and mentor teachers, making sure the practicum settings are appropriate.

In the credential program at Mills College, students receive a great deal of support from the team. The faculty get to know the students well and help them even at a personal level. Dave Donahue said: "[O]ne of my concerns has been that we don't overwhelm the students. . . . I tell them, look, it's good enough; stop, you don't have to do any more now." A lot of attention is given to students' field experiences. There is a weekly 2-hour student teaching seminar, careful selection and training of mentor teachers, and constant interaction with practicum supervisors. If a student is having trouble in the practicum, the faculty become directly involved. According to Anna Richert, the faculty continue this practicum support even into June, when classes are over and their official responsibility has ended.

In the Mid-Town program, similarly, the faculty show care to the students in a variety of ways. For example, we coordinate assignments to avoid excessive bunching; ensure that the overall assignment load is not too heavy; spend a great deal of time finding appropriate practicum placements for the students and relocating them if serious conflicts arise; visit them often in their practicum settings; help them with job hunting; and are flexible and supportive when they have personal problems. In an interview, Jennifer remarked: "It feels to me like our growth is the important thing, that we're not here just to fulfill requirements, and that we really get a lot of attention. I'd say the faculty is genuinely interested in us and in our growth, personally and professionally."

CHALLENGES TO COMMUNITY

Although we believe strongly in a community approach to preservice education, we wish to emphasize that it is not without its difficulties. While it is worthwhile and fulfilling, we wonder how many faculty (especially those who are tenure-track) will find it feasible under typical conditions. In a later chapter we will look at the need for greater institutional support for a community approach and for social constructivist programming generally. Here we simply review some of the challenges so readers are aware of them as they consider the approach.

Workload. Given the faculty commitment required, a community approach to preservice education is quite labor-intensive, leaving less time for other activities with higher status in the academy. Terry DeJong at Edith Cowan University commented:

> [T]here are downsides related to things like time and trying to meet the needs of everyone in planning. . . . These are typical difficulties in a collaborative environment. And the bottom line is hard work. You can't sit on your laurels here and expect things to happen, you have to make them happen. And you don't have a lot of time to do the things you want to as an academic: writing, research, and so on. We're creating something new every day.

Rod Chadbourne added: "[Y]ou've got to attend to detail. . . . [A] lot of what I was doing [as director] could have been done by someone less qualified. But if it isn't done . . . it starts to unravel. . . . Previously I spent that time doing research, publishing, adding to my CV." Nevertheless, the Cowan faculty felt the approach was worthwhile. Lesley Newhouse-Maiden said: "[T]here is a sense in which it is donated time, but there are dividends and I enjoy it. . . . [A]lthough it is not counted in our work, it's beneficial." And Rod observed: "I just have to accept [the consequences of allowing] teaching to occupy a higher priority."

Intensity of the program. There is a paradox with a cohort community in that despite the fact that students and faculty feel supported, pressure can develop related to trying to attain the ideals of the program. At Mills College, Dave Donahue observed:

> [T]here is something about the intensity of this program, and it could be related to being a cohort . . . because we have such good relationships with [the students] and they admire us and know we take them seriously, they all work so hard. There's a kind of competition to work harder than everybody else. And I find it in the faculty too. Like if somebody says, "Oh, I was here until 8:00 last night," rather than someone else saying, "But that's terrible, we need to get you home earlier," they say, "Well I was here all night."

Later, Dave pursued this point further: "[T]here's a different kind of competition here . . . and it's definitely a double-edged sword . . . and that's an interesting thing about community, I just don't think it's always good."

In the Mid-Town program we have noticed a similar phenomenon. Faculty who are full-time in the program and also doing doctoral thesis research often work extremely hard on the program to the neglect of their doctoral studies, not wishing to let down their students and colleagues. Among the students, too, although they know the faculty will be understanding, they sometimes put too much pressure on themselves. For example, Kathryn commented:

> I guess one of the greatest challenges [of the campus program] was the professors, the instructors within our core group; they always had so much energy and they were always so well prepared that you felt when you came in you had to offer that back. And sometimes that was a challenge, if you were tired or not feeling well.

Overall we see this situation as positive, in that people are channeling their activities toward worthwhile goals rather than just trying to be "the best" in a competitive way. However, it can create a high intensity in the program that needs to be mitigated; and how this can be done is not always clear.

Complexity of relationships. When having a supportive teacher–student relationship is emphasized, certain challenges follow. Although these may be just "part of the price" of the positive outcomes, containing the potential problems requires well-honed interpersonal skills and considerable time commitment on the part of faculty. In the Mid-Town program, for example, our closeness with the students results in stress when we have to give a student a very low grade, draw attention to unprofessional behavior, or support a mentor teacher in failing a student in the practicum. Sometimes students feel betrayed, and fellow students tend to rally to their defense whatever the facts of the case. The same phenomenon occurs where a member of the faculty team has to be spoken to for not performing well or not doing his or her share of the work. Exception is taken to the apparently illogical shift from friendly co-community member to critic and judge.

At Mills College, similarly, Dave Donahue noted the stresses and time commitment involved in faculty–student relationships within a community:

> One thing I like here is the relationship with the students; I get to learn from them. But to some extent it's tricky: I feel that my status with them is unclear. . . . I wouldn't have it any other way, but it's exhausting . . . because I have all these relationships with students and I feel so invested in them. And it's a weird relationship where we're really close, but they're going to be gone in a year; and we're really close, but they're paying $15,000 to be here. . . . And every year I have one student who I feel should not be a teacher, and that becomes really hard, given that we have these relationships, and given that we're part of a community—you know, "all for one and one for all"—and somebody isn't going to get over the bar. . . . I have two students right now I literally lose sleep over. . . . Part of me wishes we were all separate professors, and someone would just give them a poor grade and

there would be certain consequences. . . . But instead we get together and have all these meetings. . . . So it's a lot of time; but I trust the process, so I'm not nervous in that sense. But also it's emotionally draining in a way that goes beyond taking up time.

Institutional pressure to increase enrolment. Faculty in all three programs feel they may have to increase enrollment at some stage, which would undermine the cohort community and threaten the social constructivist approach. At Edith Cowan, because of local demographics, the faculty are concerned that the cohort may have to become considerably larger than 80 in the near future. At OISE/UT proposals have been made from time to time to increase class size in foundations and elective courses, both to reduce costs and to enable students to have more exposure to busy tenure-track faculty. In the interviews at Mills College, concern was expressed that the credential program might have to be enlarged for financial reasons. Near the end of her interview, Anna Richert said:

> [To a new college provost] I would say, value the community that we have and don't let us get fragmented. Help us stay together as a community. Attend to the fact that as we get bigger and bigger, we are in jeopardy of losing something that we have and don't let that happen. Find ways to hold us together. In fact, I intend to go from this meeting to one with the woman who probably will be the provost, and I probably will say something like that.

Skepticism among faculty and students. Some faculty do not appear to agree with a community emphasis, or at least do not see it as feasible in a university context. In the Mid-Town program over the years we have had difficulties with faculty who just teach their courses and leave, or who do practicum supervision but in a judgmental rather than a supportive manner. Rod Chadbourne at Edith Cowan spoke of a few faculty in the school of education who questioned the appropriateness of providing special facilities to accommodate the middle school cohort and, more generally, were "skeptical of our focus on doing things differently, with emphasis on professional community, constructivism, and integration." For the middle school team, being just one program among many and having to face such skepticism, "it wasn't such a pleasant experience."

Turning to student attitudes, Anna Richert at Mills College observed that some students have greater respect for academic and pedagogical specializations, showing only limited appreciation of the comprehensive, holistic approach to teaching advocated and embodied in the larger cohort program. In the Mid-Town program, as we have said, while virtually all students enjoy the Mid-Town community experience, some wonder whether they are learning what they need to deal with the hard realities of teaching. They see the benefits of community in terms of their well-being as *students*; however, they think a more individualistic approach, with direct transmission of content and skills, would be more efficient in preparing them to be *teachers*. This is perhaps an inconsistent outlook, but it is a reality we face.

External pressures from government and school systems. The misgivings some student teachers have about a social constructivist approach are grounded in part in the current emphasis in government and school systems on detailed curriculum coverage and testing. In this climate, there often appears to be insufficient time for the personal sharing, class celebrations, whole group and small group discussions, and other activities that ground the co-construction of knowledge. Accordingly, some students believe preservice instruction should focus rather on systematic coverage of what needs to be taught at the various grade levels and how to teach it. As one of our Mid-Town graduates said after 2 years of teaching:

> At the beginning you just want answers. You don't want someone to say "What are we going to do?" because you don't know what to do. At the beginning it's better if somebody tells you how to do it, and then once you get comfortable with that you can modify it on your own. In teachers' college they should be really specific, like "This is what you can do"; [they should give] practical information.

Beyond the school context, governments and other agencies are increasingly pressuring teacher education to go in the same direction. At Mills College, Dave Donahue commented: "[L]ast year and this year are the first years where we, as a teacher education faculty, are feeling almost the same constraints [as the teachers in schools]—the testing, top-down mandates, the deskilling of our profession." Linda Kroll said: "I try to be hopeful, but it's very discouraging in California right now; I think we'll get out of it, but it's hard, very hard." And Anna Richert observed:

> [I]n the last several years, [there's been a shift to] a highly regulated situation, especially in urban schools. Our graduates go on to Oakland schools and are regulated in the most profoundly problematic ways. The curriculum is typically scripted and [observers] . . . come around to the classroom to check that the teachers are saying particular things at particular hours and are on particular pages. This is devastating for our students. So the standardization, the standardized tests, the heightened regulation of both teaching and teacher education, all this is difficult for us.

Of course, we believe that a community approach to teacher education and schooling, if well implemented, is ultimately more effective than one characterized by skills and drills, individualism and transmission; and we think this can be demonstrated. However, much has to be done to make this model more feasible for preservice educators and others and to devise ways to show its effectiveness more clearly. Thus, while we strongly advocate a community approach, for the reasons given, we do not wish to underestimate the challenges.

CHAPTER 5

Establishing an Inclusive Approach

[W]e find a variety of ways for STEP teachers to inquire into the lives
of their students, to understand how the adolescents they teach see and
experience the world. Rather than trying to teach about race and
ethnicity in ways that stereotype individuals as representatives of
groups, we weave readings about language and culture in the context
of classrooms, schools and communities throughout courses.
    —Linda Darling-Hammond on Stanford's secondary
    preservice program, "Learning to Teach for Social Justice"

The discussion of community in the previous chapter provides a natural entry
into the topic of inclusive preservice education. We believe that building community is the single most important means of fostering inclusive attitudes and
practices among student teachers. However, there are other key elements as
well, such as explicit inquiry into difference, equity, and inclusion; infusion of
an inclusive orientation throughout the program; personal construction of an
inclusive orientation by student teachers; and various kinds of direct experience
of difference, exclusion, and inclusion in educational settings and beyond.

    Why should one adopt an inclusive approach in preservice education? As
suggested in chapter 1, we believe that such an approach to teaching and
learning is fundamental to a social constructivist position. If we wish to have
the other benefits of social constructivism, we must embrace inclusion: it
comes with the territory. This is apart from other moral and emotional reasons we may have for ensuring that all our students are respected and equi-
tably treated. The emphasis in social constructivism on community, social
learning, critical inquiry, recognition of "the other," personal construction of
knowledge, and holism all point in the direction of inclusion.

    All the preservice programs profiled in earlier chapters have a strong inclu-
sion orientation. For example, at Mills College the six principles that guide the
credential program all come under the umbrella of equity and justice, and from
the beginning of the program—notably, at the orientation retreat—the equity
implications of the principles are explored. And in the Teachers College elementary program one of the main assignments is an intensive child study that
Lin Goodwin, director of the program, has described as helping student teachers "resist inclinations to 'otherize' culturally, linguistically, and academically

diverse children, and come to recognize the commonalities they share with them" (Goodwin, 2002, pp. 137–38).

The term inclusion in this chapter is used as an umbrella for a related group of concepts: inclusion itself, equity, social justice, recognition of difference, respect for others, gender equity, multiculturalism, antiracism, and so on. Our decision to use the word inclusion to represent this group is to some extent arbitrary: several other terms could serve this purpose. However, we favor inclusion because it is widely used among writers and practitioners in the field, has a strong difference and equity connotation, suggests a key role for community, and has a more inviting ring than some other terms.

With respect to this last point, it is often noted that student teachers sometimes react negatively—at least initially—to discussion of issues of difference and inclusion (Irvine, 2003; Vavrus, 2002). Accordingly, it is important to indicate from the outset that we are going to work *with* student teachers in this area rather than in top-down mode; and the word inclusion sends this message. We will discuss in detail later why we believe a largely non-authoritarian approach is legitimate and indeed necessary for progress in matters of inclusion. Suffice it to say here that, as with other areas of learning, inclusion cannot be effectively taught in a transmission manner: students must be actively engaged in constructing an inclusive approach to teaching and learning, taking ownership of it as a concern.

What types of difference are addressed by the concept of inclusion? The range is a wide one. We agree with Melnick and Zeichner (1997) that "an adequate definition of 'diversity' needs to be broad and inclusive." These authors focus especially on "social class, race, ethnicity, and language" in their 1997 chapter, but they say that attention must also be given to "gender, age, religion, exceptionalities, sexual orientation, etc." (p. 25). We believe that such a comprehensive approach is justified because bias of all these kinds has a negative impact in the lives of many people. Furthermore, one only fully grasps the point of an inclusive approach when one sees that it applies to all types of prejudice and discrimination. Everyone must be included in the classroom. As Villegas and Lucas (2002) say, "student diversity is central to the learning process," and this view of learning must be "at the heart of teacher preparation" (p. xxii).

In focusing on diversity and inclusion, however, we should be wary of stereotyping, which can result in our doing more harm than good. Irvine (2003) observes that "inadequate or cursory knowledge can lead to more, not less, hostility and stereotyping toward culturally different students" (p. 16). Melnick and Zeichner (1997) report that "at times, teacher education practices designed to combat negative stereotypes actually reinforce teacher candidates' prejudices and misconceptions about diverse students" (p. 29). A concern expressed often by members of minority and disadvantaged groups is that they are not recognized and treated as "ordinary" human beings. This does not mean that all individuals and groups are the same: on the contrary, there are enormous differences in interests, tastes, temperament, and so on. However, student teachers need to realize that diversity exists *within* groups even more than between them; and that people from different groups have a great many more *commonalities* than differences: the vast majority of human differences simply do not run along racial, ethnic, gender, age, or other subgroup lines. Irvine (2003) stresses the need to foster awareness of "the shared interests and connections of all people in the world," as well as the differences (p. 17). And Darling-Hammond (2002a), speaking about the STEP program at Stanford, observes:

> Students conduct case studies of individual students, observing, interviewing, and shadowing them to better understand their lives and learning. . . . Because STEP teachers complete a full year of student teaching while they are taking courses, they always have the opportunity to apply what they are learning directly to the classroom in real time. This helps to prevent concerns about race, class, and culture from becoming objectified, oversimplified, or an abstraction that could result mostly in "otherizing" students. (p. 4)

A COMMUNAL SETTING FOR LEARNING TO BE INCLUSIVE

An essential early step in establishing an inclusive preservice program is to build a cohort community, as described in the previous chapter. According to Darling-Hammond (2002b),

> consciously creating community from the sharing of multiple voices is one of the first jobs of a teacher education program. . . . Finding space for reflection and discourse about who we are, individually and collectively, in relation to one another and to society at large creates the initial foundation for all the other necessary work on social justice. (p. 203)

Similarly, Irvine (2003) maintains that "the successful implementation of a multicultural curriculum [in teacher education] should be preceded by systemic climate and culture change" (p. 16). Vavrus (2002) speaks of the need for teacher educators "to create learning communities that allow a rich investigation into topics surrounding multicultural education purposes" (p. 149).

Why is community so crucial? To begin, establishing such a community in the program models inclusive pedagogy. It takes us beyond lectures, reading, and discussion and allows students to see firsthand what is involved in running an inclusive classroom. As Irvine says, a mere "curriculum approach to multicultural education requires students to make critical applications and transfers without appropriate guidance" (p. 17). The modeling also sends a clear message that the faculty are serious about inclusion, that their advocacy is not just rhetoric. They are so convinced of the importance of inclusion that they are willing to put a great deal of time and energy into achieving it, taking on all the challenges of this kind of programming in a university setting. Further, it shows students that they will be supported in applying this approach themselves, both on campus and in the practicum. Vavrus (2002) comments: "Preservice teachers organized into learning community cohorts . . . can come to see their faculty members as co-learners with them in the quest to understand and actualize multicultural education reform" (p. 152).

An inclusive cohort community also gives students an experience of inclusive living. Many student teachers come to their preservice program with little personal knowledge of diverse environments, whether at home or in school (Darling-Hammond, 2002a; Melnick & Zeichner, 1997; Villegas & Lucas, 2002). In their previous academic work at the university level, specifically, although they may have taken classes with students of varied backgrounds they will not typically have had much close interaction with them because of the impersonal nature of much university education. Student teachers need to experience what an inclusive community is like and have the opportunity to embrace such a way of being and practice it over a significant period. There is reason to believe that, given the experience, student teachers will respond very positively. According to Villegas & Lucas (2002), a large proportion of those who enter teaching do so with a strong desire "to make a difference in the lives of young people. This commitment is a resource teacher educators can draw on" (p. xix).

In particular, a cohort community provides an opportunity to learn what "others" are like: that they are human beings like themselves, that they can often be "kindred spirits" to a greater extent than some people whose background they share, that there is great diversity within a given group, and so on. Of course, students will have had some experiences of this kind before; and the full range of cultures, races, and so on will certainly not be present in their preservice cohort, given its small size and relatively specialized purpose. Nevertheless, if a close community is created in the program it will be a key learning experience from this point of view.

Another reason why community is essential is because it provides a safe environment for discussion of issues of equity and inclusion. This was a recurring theme in the programs described in earlier chapters. For example, as noted in chapter 4, Linda Kroll at Mills College commented that "[i]f you're going to talk about issues of social justice, equity, and excellence . . . then you have to have a safe place. . . . So . . . the first thing you have to do is establish a community in your classroom." Similarly, Vavrus (2002) observes that a learning community affords "a setting that allows the investigation of thorny yet crucial multicultural education issues" (p. 143). In our own program at OISE/UT we have found that, later in the year when the community has become solidly established, most minority and nonminority students are remarkably willing to share their experiences and views in this area.

Finally, community in the program is important because, as discussed in chapter 4, learning is in large part a social matter. To a significant extent the whole group must come to see the appropriateness of an inclusive approach, since ideas on such matters tend to be mutually reinforcing. Darling-Hammond (2002b) comments:

> The journey toward these understandings [of equity pedagogy] is intensely personal, and yet it is necessarily social—it has to be conducted in the company of others who teach us about their own experiences and who learn with us about how to build a common understanding that is greater than the sum of its parts. (p. 202)

She notes Dewey's statement that in order to have "values in common," members of a group must have "a large variety of shared undertakings and experiences" (Dewey, 1916/1966, p. 84 quoted in Darling-Hammond, 2002b, p. 202).

In closing this section, it should be mentioned that careful student selection is important for the success of a community-based approach to inclusive preservice preparation. On the one hand, we need *a diverse student body* so the community experience is as rich an example as possible of inclusive education, and so students can learn firsthand about the lives and views of people of different backgrounds. On the other hand, it is important to admit *students who are open to an inclusive approach* and will work well together in honing such an approach (Melnick & Zeichner, 1997; Villegas & Lucas, 2002). While drawing on the experiences of members of minority groups within the cohort, however, we should not forget that they are a small and select group whose experiences may not be typical. Also, we must always ensure that they do not feel pressured to go beyond their comfort zone in sharing their views. We have found that sometimes minority students do not reach a point, even by the end of the program, where they wish to talk much about their own experiences and views with respect to equity matters: their greater concern, for the present at least, is to be accepted as an "ordinary" member of the cohort community.

INQUIRY INTO DIFFERENCE, EQUITY, AND INCLUSION

While much can be learned about inclusion through the cohort community, it is still essential to have explicit, critical study of issues of diversity and inclusion. Social constructivism is sometimes seen as advocating a purely personal journey, whereas in fact it assumes extensive learning from other people's ideas. Piaget emphasized the importance of exposure to the views of peers, and Vygotsky stressed the impact of the teacher, along with broader sociocultural influences. Although individuals must modify and interpret ideas gained from other sources and develop their own distinctive approach, without the benefit of such input their own ideas would be entirely inadequate. This is true with respect to knowledge in subject areas such as science and mathematics (Brophy, 2002), and equally with regard to more general sociocultural and pedagogical matters.

Several bodies of knowledge need to be studied in inclusive preservice education. *Poststructuralist and postmodernist ideas* of the kind discussed in chapter 1 are especially relevant. Student teachers should be aware of recent thought about how ideology pervades popular culture (Barthes) and how formal knowledge is molded by the interests of dominant groups (Lyotard and Foucault). They must be cognizant of the way "the other" is distorted, suppressed, or often just ignored by popular culture and academic disciplines (Derrida). They need to be disabused of assumptions about there being just one truth or "center" of thought that is universal and unchanging, namely, the establishment metanarratives (Lyotard and Rorty). And they should learn how even oppressed groups themselves often internalize ideology-based beliefs held about them (Freire, Gramsci).

Student teachers also need to be exposed to *relatively factual information* about diverse groups, matters on which widespread ignorance and misunderstanding exists. Goodwin (1997) states that multicultural teacher education should "disturb" the beliefs that many student teachers bring with them to the program. Among other things, students "need to understand the historical and sociopolitical context of education and race in this country. The school experiences of children of color in America cannot be divorced from this painful and inequitable legacy" (pp. 16–17). Irvine (2003) speaks of having to combat the "sincere fictions" that student teachers often have with regard to minority students, for example, their "negative beliefs and low expectations of success for such students" (pp. xv–xvi). Delpit (1995) notes that prospective teachers are too often "exposed to descriptions of failure rather than models of success. We expose student teachers to an education that relies upon name calling and labeling ('disadvantaged,' 'at-risk,' 'learning disabled,' 'the underclass') to explain its failures" (pp. 177–78). She proposes instead that we "make available to our teacher initiates the many success stories about educating poor children and children of color . . . [and] make sure that they learn about those teachers who are quietly going about the job of producing excellence in educating poor and culturally diverse students" (p. 178).

Beyond offering factual information, an inclusive preservice program should ensure consideration of *theory of culture and multiculturalism*. In order to break down monolithic and static views of culture, sustained discussion is needed of diversity within cultures, commonalities across cultures, and how cultures change over time. The advantages and disadvantages of changes such as globalization and other forms of cultural assimilation should be explored. Systematic inquiry is needed into the ways in which diversity plays a positive role in society, and how different cultures often have equally good ways of achieving the same ends, thus calling into question the view of difference as "problem" or "deficit" (Cochran-Smith, Davis, & Fries, 2004, p. 949). At a personal level, students should become aware of how much one can learn from people of other cultures, how multicultural skills can increase our interpersonal skills, and how individuals must typically develop their own way of life to some extent, resisting pressure to conform entirely to the norms of their particular group(s).

Further, *traditional questions in ethics and political theory* need to be explored: issues of equality, justice, self-interest, altruism, and social responsibility. These are complex and controversial topics on which a great deal has been written. There is no point ignoring the fact that opinion varies on whether, or to what extent, one should treat everyone equally or favor oneself and one's inner group. Virtually everyone in fact favors themselves or their own group, and solid argument is needed on these matters if one is not to be dismissed as an ideologue or dreamer. Rorty (1989) takes these issues seriously, and argues that we must find ways to see others—perhaps *all* others—as members of our "we-group" if we are to give due place to their needs.

While inquiry into all these areas is necessary in a preservice program, the manner in which it is carried out is of crucial importance. We will argue later that, on the whole, it should not be done in separate courses but rather infused throughout the program. The point we wish to emphasize here is that, as far as possible, theoretical inquiry related to inclusion should be integrated with discussion of practical matters. In our Mid-Town program we have found that student teachers, with just 9 months to prepare for having their own classroom, do not have a great deal of patience for pure theory on matters of equity and inclusion (or any other topic). They want to know "how to do it." And although we resist the notion than one can have good practice without solid theory, we accept that theory is usually best acquired in the context of practice. This is again a social constructivist tenet. So in all our courses we immediately illustrate theoretical points by reference to practical strategies. For example, in addressing gender bias in School & Society, intense inquiry into gender issues is combined with watching videos of classroom interaction and discussing practical ways to ensure that girls and boys receive equal attention in the classroom.

INFUSING AN INCLUSIVE ORIENTATION THROUGHOUT THE PROGRAM

Rationale for an infusion approach. While inclusion must be an explicit focus of a preservice program, much of the work in this area should be infused throughout the program rather than conducted separately (Darling-Hammond, 2002a; Irvine, 2003; Vavrus, 2002). According to Cochran-Smith, Davis, and Fries (2004), "the conceptual literature asserts that coherence may well be the most critical aspect of multicultural teacher education" (p. 961). Villegas and Lucas (2002) advocate a coherent, infused approach, introducing it as follows:

To successfully move the field beyond the fragmented and superficial treatment of diversity that currently prevails, we teacher educators need to reconceptualize our approach to educating teachers. . . . A salient aspect of this work involves placing issues of diversity at the center of . . . the learning experiences offered to prospective teachers not only in education courses but also in arts and sciences courses and in field experiences and practica in communities and schools. We contend that without conceptual coherence across these learning experiences . . . prospective teachers may never see the relationships among key ideas or make the connections between theory and practice they will need to become effective teachers. (p. xiv)

If inclusion is only discussed separately from the rest of the program, it tends to be viewed as tokenism or an "add-on" by student teachers and not taken seriously; and, as Villegas and Lucas say, its theoretical significance and implications for practice may not be understood. Issues of equity and social justice, in our view, fall within the broader field of values, and in values education generally a separate course approach has not been found to be very effective (Beck & Kosnik, 1998). This is in line with Dewey's (1909/1975) observation that "the influence of direct moral instruction, even at its very best, is *comparatively* small in amount and slight in influence, when the whole field of moral growth through education is taken into account" (p. 4).

Earlier we talked about how learning to be inclusive and teach inclusively should be infused into the cohort community experience. Here we discuss ways of integrating inclusion into coursework, practicum experiences, and activities that involve both coursework and the practicum. We do so primarily by presenting examples from preservice programs at the University of California–Berkeley and Wheelock College, programs that we regard as social constructivist in nature and that Vavrus (2002) identifies as ones that "infuse multicultural concepts and internships throughout the curriculum for their respective teacher candidates" (p. 99).

Conditions for infusion. Before describing these programs, we wish to note that infusion of an inclusive approach in preservice education is greatly aided by three conditions: careful selection of students, appointment of suitable faculty, and institutional support. As noted earlier, having a high proportion of minority students in a program provides a major resource for gaining insight into multicultural realities; it also helps ensure (though does not guarantee) that issues of equity and inclusion are constantly addressed. In addition, *all* students in the program, whether of minority membership or not, should as far as possible be ones who are interested in and disposed to an inclusive approach to teaching. Melnick and Zeichner (1997) speak of the need to "determine potential abilities necessary for successful cross-cultural teachers" and advocate that we "focus more on picking the right people rather than changing the wrong ones" (p. 27). This may sound harsh, but on the one hand the well-being of many future generations of school students is at stake; and on the other, we are not doing candidates a favor by admitting them to a profession to which they are not suited. Furthermore, standard admissions practice involves trying to select teacher candidates who have the potential to be talented teachers, and many of the qualities we look for are precisely the ones needed for inclusive teaching: being child-centered, caring, responsible, observant, flexible, able to individualize instruction, interested in the home–school connection, socially and politically aware, and skilled in communication and social interaction.

Selection of faculty who are inclusive in outlook is also important, especially in an integrated program involving joint planning, team teaching, close attention to the practicum, and ongoing development of a coherent multicultural approach. Vavrus (2002) states that an infusion approach requires faculty with "multicultural competence" (p. 157) who "value the importance of multicultural education reform and hold an academic interest in diversity issues, interdisciplinary scholarship, and collaborative teaching and learning" (pp. 159–60). The hiring of appropriate faculty in turn calls for strong institutional support, which is important for other reasons as well. "To restructure a teacher education program for multicultural education reform takes institutional commitment and cooperation" (Vavrus, 2002, p. 160). A supportive institution in this area ensures a general climate of inclusion and provision of resources needed for "faculty deliberations, development of action plans, implementation, and evaluation" (p. 160).

University of California–Berkeley

UC–Berkeley's Developmental Teacher Education (DTE) Program is a 2-year elementary master's program with a focus on "enhancing students' abilities to work effectively with learners and parents from increasingly diverse communities" (Snyder, 2000, p. 141). It attempts to do this by infusing a multicultural approach throughout the program. With a dedicated, caring staff and only 20 to 25 students enrolled in each of the 2 years, a close cohort community can be established, thus facilitating joint work on inclusive teaching. A high proportion of racial minority candidates are enrolled in the program (50% in 1995–1997) and the faculty are committed to continuing to increase this number and also the number from low socioeconomic backgrounds (Snyder, 2000, p. 141).

The program has strong support from the school of education and the university generally. According to Snyder (2000), "the first thing one sees upon entering the Education Building is a large bulletin board outside the Dean's office showcasing the work of DTE teacher education students through the work of the students in their classrooms" (p. 119). Senior level tenured faculty do much of the teaching in the program; many rich learning resources are available in the university, such as the media center and the science education center; and the university pays the practicum supervisors exceptionally well (p. 119).

Several courses in the program integrate a major multicultural component. For example, Education in Inner Cities "alerts students to the challenges of urban settings, particularly those challenges related to race and class. In addition, the course allows students to begin to access and understand their own stereotypes and prejudices in a non-threatening environment" (p. 114). Later in the program, the course Teaching Linguistic and Cultural Minority Students provides "opportunities for students to construct practical answers to the questions they began asking . . . in the Education in Inner Cities course— specifically, what can a teacher do about the gnarly issues of race, class, and first- and second-language development in classrooms, schools, communities, and the educational 'system'?" (p. 118).

Just as influential as the courses, however, is the program's "deep, consistent, profound, and sustaining centering on children and how they develop" (p. 127), which helps foster an inclusive approach to teaching. In each of the 4 semesters of the program there is a "core seminar" on human development, the purpose of which is "to provide teachers with sufficient background to understand, and hence to value, the activities of each child in the classroom. . . . Of particular importance is the effort to combine social and moral development with an understanding of psychological development" (Snyder, 2000, p. 107). As one instructor said:

> When the content of school is related to children's experiences it becomes a tool to raise issues that are important to young people as they try to understand themselves and others. In this way, content raises important social and ethical issues such as building empathy and understanding for diverse others, and it provides examples of good people trying to be better in the context of human interactions. (Snyder, 2000, p. 115)

The inclusion emphasis is also seen in the field experiences. Practicum schools and placements are chosen to provide students with a diversity of experiences and an opportunity to implement what they are discussing on campus about equity and inclusion. Coursework and practica are closely coordinated. For example, the fifth placement includes "a focus on individual children, especially English language learning children, to complement the course Teaching Linguistic and Cultural Minority Students also taken this semester" (p. 117). And throughout the program, a weekly student-teaching seminar is held to facilitate reflection on their classroom experiences. The seminar provides workshops on "teaching related issues" including, for example, "cross-cultural communication" (pp. 110–11).

Wheelock College

Wheelock College's 4-year undergraduate program in Early Childhood Care and Education integrates inclusion in many of the same ways as the Berkeley program. The mission of the college is "the improvement of the quality of life for children and their families" (Miller & Silvernail, 2000, p. 68), and the college is "firmly rooted in a developmental point of view" (p. 69). As stated by the president: "Everything grows from the child. You are the curriculum builders. You watch, you look, and you see, you create. You allow the child to create. Methods are not so important as the child. The child comes first" (p. 69).

In the Wheelock program, each student teacher chooses one of 4 *subject-matter* majors, and all 4 "are conceived in multicultural perspective and offer a variety of multicultural courses and experiences" (p. 71). Turning to *pedagogic* study, several courses have a multicultural emphasis, such as Curriculum Development for Inclusive Early Childhood Settings, Multicultural Teaching and Learning Strategies, and Curriculum Design for Inclusive Elementary Education Programs. In these courses, students learn "to understand and value the diversity of student backgrounds and the integrity of cultures other than their own" (p. 78). The program's *field experiences* take place largely in multicultural and special needs settings, have similar goals to the campus courses, and are closely integrated with the campus courses. This integration is aided by the fact that all the campus faculty participate in practicum supervision. The weekly practicum seminar, which is team-taught, links the practicum with the campus program and serves further to relate theory to practice and reinforce the basic themes of the program.

Of special interest in the Wheelock program is the fact that its child development emphasis has been reinterpreted over the years so that it now overlaps extensively with its inclusion emphasis. This has happened at Berkeley too, but at Wheelock the shift is talked about more explicitly. As Miller and Silvernail (2000) explain:

> At Wheelock the understanding of human development extends beyond the traditional notion of individual movement through a sequence of stages. Rather, the concept is broadened to include the diverse influences that affect learning and development. Students learn to look at children in the context of their families, communities, and cultures. They are encouraged to develop sensitivity to differences and a multicultural awareness. (pp. 79–80)

The student teachers refer to this concept of developmentalism as the "Wheelock Way," and see it as having the following dimensions (among others):

- Learning from one's students and developing curriculum from knowledge of students, families, and cultures.
- Constructing curriculum as interests and needs emerge; being flexible, responsive, and resourceful.
- Knowing how to observe and listen to children.
- Being sensitive to diversity and knowing how to teach multiculturally.
- Being comfortable about advocating for inclusion.
- Identifying and working on student strengths. (p. 86)

We have here, then, a high level of infusion of inclusiveness into preservice education. The approach identified as the heart and direction of the program, namely, developmentalism, is defined in such a way that it is *also* an inclusive, multicultural approach. Miller and Silvernail (2000) report that "the human development perspective . . . has been modified and adapted to meet the needs of a more complex and multicultural society. The faculty and administration take seriously their commitment to urban children and their families. . . . As the undergraduate dean explains, 'Education is more than cognitive development. The paradigm has shifted to include social, emotional, and affective issues as well. We have to include race, class, and identity'" (p. 100). This does not mean that the human development focus is negated or diluted. Rather, its *essential* connection in contemporary society to an inclusive approach to teaching and learning is revealed and emphasized.

PERSONAL CONSTRUCTION OF
AN INCLUSIVE ORIENTATION

While there should be explicit advocacy and discussion of an inclusive approach, and infusion of this approach throughout the program, ultimately student teachers must take ownership of their development in this domain. This is essential if our treatment of the area is to be social constructivist in nature. It is self-defeating to be authoritarian and moralistic with respect to equity and inclusion while recommending an inquiry approach in the rest of the program. A top-down transmission pedagogy with regard to inclusive teaching, or in any area, stifles motivation and intelligent pursuit of goals. Our efforts should be directed toward ensuring that inclusion becomes something that appeals to students, interests them, and makes sense to them, something they commit themselves to and implement under their own steam. Otherwise they may quickly abandon it when exposed to the rigors of the practicum and their first years of teaching.

Schoonmaker (2002) relates how, within a social constructivist preservice program strongly committed to inclusion (the Teachers College elementary cohort program described in chapter 3), she and her colleagues support student teachers' construction of their own approach to teaching. Early in her book, she notes that "[i]n far too many cases, teacher preparation does not seem to have a lasting effect," and she suggests that the reason is the failure of preservice programs to build on the ideas students bring to the program. In her view, knowledge about teaching "must be co-constructed if it is to have lasting meaning" (p. x). Schoonmaker then presents in detail the case of "Kay," a student teacher who is encouraged to build on her prior understanding of teaching (while also being exposed to extensive discussion of equity and inclusion). She notes that as Kay develops her approach to teaching, she increasingly "analyzes events and assesses consequences with reference to moral and ethical criteria," including the "moral" criterion of inclusiveness. "Equity, fairness, and justice are clear themes that begin to appear in [Kay's] journal entries *around the borders of her more compelling practical concerns*" (pp. 55–56; emphasis added).

From an equity perspective, the priority Kay gives to the "more compelling practical concerns" of a beginning teacher may seem inappropriate, and at a certain level it is. However, Schoonmaker suggests that tolerance of such an emphasis in the early stages is justified: we must often accept this phase in teachers' development in the interests of ensuring their long-term growth in an inclusive approach. "The focus of student teachers on themselves and their relationship with cooperating teachers, students, and the curriculum tends to preclude serious and penetrating, deliberative rationality, even though they may be motivated by social concerns" (p. 57). She concurs with Kagan's (1992) view that "the initial focus on self appears to be a necessary and crucial element in the first stage of teacher development," and "attempts by supervisors to shorten or abort a student teacher's period of inward focus may be counterproductive" (Kagan, 1992, p. 155; Schoonmaker, 2002, p. 57).

Similarly, Vavrus (2002) advocates supporting student teachers in constructing their own approach to inclusive teaching. He proposes that they be prepared within a "learning community" that allows them "to investigate challenging multicultural issues in collaboration with their peers and faculty" (p. 161). He believes that the traditional transmission approach to teacher education undermines inclusive pedagogy because it reinforces the idea that there is one "truth," namely that of the dominant culture. In a learning community model, by contrast,

> hierarchical roles between teacher educators and preservice and inservice teachers are significantly reduced . . . faculty shift their approach to that of facilitators for teacher education student learning while simultaneously becoming co-learners with their students in a democratic, caring community. . . . Multiple perspectives are encouraged . . . as education students construct their own understandings and knowledge about multicultural education. (p. 161)

While adhering to a developmental, constructivist pedagogy, however, preservice faculty should feel free to state explicitly their own views about equity and inclusion. Indeed, this is essential for stimulating the development of student teachers' ideas (and for testing and refining the instructors' ideas). Sometimes it is suggested that instructors should keep their opinions to themselves—*especially* in moral and cultural areas—in order to avoid indoctrination. However, on the contrary, indoctrination is more likely to occur if teachers try to hide their views, since students quickly figure out what their views are but lack the opportunity to assess them in an open, systematic manner.

Indoctrination is avoided not by refraining from expressing our opinions but rather by creating a classroom setting in which students have time—and encouragement—to discuss, disagree, propose alternatives, and ultimately develop their own point of view (Beck, 1990, 1993). As Vavrus (2002) says, "teacher education reform necessitates fundamental institutional restructuring [resulting in] a balance between deepening multicultural content knowledge and creating teacher candidate time for necessary attitudinal expression, exploration, and development" (p. 165).

LEARNING ABOUT INCLUSION THROUGH EXPERIENCE

Experience-based learning is fundamental to social constructivism, and a key aspect of social constructivist preservice education is utilization of students' experiences of life and education gained prior to and during the program. With respect to equity and inclusion, appropriate experiences during the program can expose student teachers to types of diversity, prejudice, and disadvantage not encountered before. They can also give them the opportunity to build on their prior experiences and modify their existing ideas in this area. We have already discussed the role of the cohort community experience in fostering an inclusive approach to teaching. Two other sets of experiences frequently mentioned in the literature are those occurring in the practicum and in the community beyond the school.

Experiences in the practicum. In order to hone their philosophy of inclusion and their skills in this area, student teachers need practicum placements in schools with a diverse student body. Preservice programs often go to considerable lengths to provide opportunities of this kind. We have seen this already in the case of the programs at UC–Berkeley and Wheelock College. A similar example is found in the STEP program at Stanford, where the interviewees in our study spoke of their commitment to selecting partner schools with a diverse student population. They discussed the difficulty that arises if one of these schools has a tracking system that is incompatible with the program's commitment to helping minority students achieve at a high academic level. Because of the program's philosophy, STEP student teachers are usually placed in the lower-track classrooms in such a school, where they can give valuable support to teachers or departments working for reform. Darling-Hammond (2002a) notes that in recent years STEP has made significant advances in developing "professional development school relationships with middle and high schools that have been working explicitly on an equity agenda. Increasingly, the kind of schooling STEP teachers observe is schooling that seeks to confront the long-standing barriers created by tracking, poor teaching, narrow curriculum, and unresponsive systems" (p. 5).

Experiences in the community beyond the school.   Direct experience of diverse communities beyond the school is widely advocated as a way of enabling student teachers to learn about diversity, inclusion, and related matters. Cochran-Smith, Davis, and Fries (2004) comment that "a particularly promising teacher preparation pedagogy appears to be community-based experience, which offers teacher candidates new understandings about culture, families, and ways of life that are different from their own" (p. 964). Boyle-Baise (2002) states that "[p]reservice teachers from all groups need more knowledge of and direct contact with people different from themselves" (p. xi); she proposes the incorporation of "multicultural service learning" into preservice programs. Villegas and Lucas (2002) discuss the nature and goals of such learning:

> Service learning is a way of organizing the content and pedagogy of a course so that community service is integrated into academic content, thus enhancing it. . . . When incorporated into courses for prospective teachers, service learning can increase their awareness and challenge their assumptions by giving them experience in contexts of cultural diversity and poverty, increasing their understanding of and appreciation for the complexities of others' lives. (p. 140)

Irvine (2003), however, while also advocating what she calls "cultural-immersion experiences," points out some of the challenges of this approach. She cautions that such experiences "should not be seen as a panacea for teacher education" (p. 84). To be successful, "they require knowledgeable, sensitive faculty in teacher education departments who want to incorporate immersion experiences into their programs" (p. 84). She also notes that such experiences take a lot of time to organize and implement and can involve considerable transportation costs. Furthermore, unless local assistance and support are available, "there may be resistance and hostility among members of the ethnic communities" (p. 84).

In general, direct cultural experiences must occur against a background of systematic and sophisticated inquiry. Such inquiry is needed to help student teachers interpret what they observe, and to give them a more comprehensive understanding of the field. Direct experience by itself, especially over a short period of time, can result in stereotyping and superficial understanding: poor people are like this, ethnic group X lives like that. Immersion experiences, then, should be viewed largely as case studies in cultural learning, illustrating general theory and providing an opportunity for student teachers to acquire skills needed for *lifelong* learning in this area.

CHAPTER 6

Having Influence and Gaining Support Beyond the Program

> [W]e must resist attempts to reduce teacher education reform to one or two factors. For example, we must recognize that the "problem" of reform has political and institutional roots.
> —Alan Tom, *Redesigning Teacher Education*

So far in this book we have focused mainly on small cohort programs with enrollments between 40 and 80. While the University of Sydney's MTeach program is relatively large, much of our attention has been on the small groupings within it. And in OISE/UT's extensive elementary preservice enterprise, we have concentrated on the Mid-Town cohort program, which enrolls just 65 student teachers. But no program is an island; and we must turn now to look at the institutional context within which cohort programs function. Support from the school, college, or department of education (SCDE), and at times the university as a whole, is very important if social constructivist programming is to be feasible. In this chapter we consider why cohort programs need broader institutional connections and support and how these may be achieved.

   As the title of this chapter suggests, part of what is involved in gaining support for our social constructivist program is to influence the larger institution in the same direction. But spreading isolated innovations in education is notoriously difficult; Sarason (1990) has detailed the many barriers to this type of change. To add this task to the already demanding role of faculty in innovative cohort programs may seem futile at best, sadistic at worst. However, we teacher educators have little choice. Although the task is daunting, if we do not win acceptance for our approach in other parts of the institution we will have difficulty maintaining it even in our own program.

   Few writers on preservice education have addressed in depth the institutional structures needed for programs of the type we are advocating. Alan Tom is the main one who has, and we will refer often to his landmark 1997 book *Redesigning Teacher Education*. According to Tom (1997) there has been "a flurry of books" on teacher education reform since the late 1980s, but many of them "are narrowly conceived. . . . [They] often ignore or give minimal attention to such issues as programmatic structure, institutional context, and change strategies" (p. 1). An obvious exception is Goodlad's writing, especially his 1990 and 1994 books, which Tom highlights. However, even these tend to lack the degree of specificity required (Tom, 1997; Wisniewski, 1990). Tom comments:

> Above all else, we must resist attempts to reduce teacher education reform to one or two factors. For example, we must recognize that the "problem" of reform has political and institutional roots, not just intellectual and conceptual ones. . . . [W]e teacher educators need to establish a basis for socially negotiating collective answers to the diverse facets of teacher education reform. . . . We teacher educators do need to change, but change is also needed in our work settings, in the way the schools and universities are linked, and in a variety of other arenas. (p. 2)

Such talk of "socially negotiating collective answers" has a strongly social constructivist flavor, and we see here that integration, inquiry, and community are as important at the institutional level as they are in individual cohorts.

Not only is there a dearth of writing about the institutional context of preservice programs, there is also a shortage of exemplars of social constructivist programs with strong institutional connections and support. Some programs—for example, at Bank Street College, Mills College, and Wheelock College—operate in a relatively small institution that is hospitable to their philosophy and where competition with specialist departments and non-preservice graduate programs is minimal. However, these are very much in the minority. Goodlad (1990b), in his extensive study of U.S. preservice programs, found that even in small liberal arts colleges teacher education typically faces the traditional challenge of lack of community, coherence, and support.

In larger universities, similarly, exemplary preservice programs usually seem to have pulled themselves up by their own bootstraps, without much understanding or encouragement on the part of the SCDE and university. Exceptions again are found, for example at Stanford and UC–Berkeley, where the preservice programs are supported and celebrated and substantial involvement of specialist tenure-track faculty is evident in both teaching and supervision. However, the preservice programs here are relatively small and not a major drain on faculty and resources. Larger programs typically encounter many difficulties.

In our discussion in this chapter of how to develop a more hospitable context for small cohort programs, we will draw examples especially from our own institution, the school (or "faculty," as it is called) of education that is OISE/University of Toronto. We do so partly because we know the case so well, but also because ours is a very large school of education (1300 preservice students, 2100 non-preservice graduate students, 6000 continuing education students) with all the traditional challenges of preservice education in such a setting. It is also one in which extensive work has been done to try to integrate preservice cohort programs with each other and secure support for them from the larger institution. Additional initiatives are still needed at OISE/UT in terms of support for preservice education: it is a work in progress. However, along with Goodlad (1990a, 1990b) and Tom (1997) we find achievement is rare in this area, and so we must cite cases of moderate success until more developed examples become available.

WHY GO BEYOND THE COHORT PROGRAM?

Why is it important to go beyond the small cohort program and address the institutional context of preservice education in SCDEs and universities? In the first place, most teachers are prepared in large programs, SCDEs, and universities, and accordingly the renewal of teacher education requires coming to terms with this reality. If a social constructivist approach to teaching and teacher education is to be widely achieved, we must find ways to implement it in large institutions where many hundreds of student teachers are gaining their qualification together. Although small social constructivist programs may be the key, as we believe they are, we must be able to establish many of them within the same university.

Another reason for attending to larger institutional matters is because a small cohort program, no matter how well planned and organized, is dependent on the SCDE (and often the university in general) in a number of ways: for adequate space, support staff, and other resources, appropriate faculty hiring and student admissions, due reward of faculty, equitable workload, suitable graduate student instructors, and so on. Unless the institution as a whole is on board in these matters, the effectiveness of the small program will be seriously reduced and its long-term viability may be threatened. Winitzky, Stoddart, and O'Keefe (1992) comment that, in the past, responsibility for innovations along these lines has rested on a small number of faculty. They speculate that, where the innovations have failed, it may have been because this small band of teacher educators "simply ran out of energy" (p. 16).

Apart from resources, hiring, reward structures, and the like, less tangible factors are also important such as moral support and the valuing of teaching and teacher education. Tom (1997) cites the case of an entirely viable preservice program that was closed down precisely because it was successful. A professor at the institution commented: "When it competed too effectively with graduate program interests, we killed it off" (p. 221). But even if a program survives, lack of concern for teacher preparation, teachers, and school related matters can have a demoralizing effect on both faculty and students in a preservice program.

Connections to the larger institution are also important because the cohort program needs the theoretical insights and other contributions of the specialist areas. A preservice program in isolation from the rest of the SCDE cannot fulfill its function adequately. According to Tom (1997), there must be constant dialogue between clinical preservice faculty and faculty from specialist fields. To further this end, he envisages creating faculty teams that "bring faculty members from diverse specializations into intimate and continuing contact with one another" (p. 213). Dagenais and Wideen (1999), in describing the multiple cohort programs at Simon Fraser University, in which "faculty associates" from the field and tenure-track faculty work closely together, document the tensions that sometimes arise for the two types of staff; however, they conclude that "[t]he bridging of university and school cultures in this program has worked well on many occasions and has led to excellence in teacher education" (p. 180).

Finally, support from the larger institution is needed at the level of the school system and government. For example, although many cohort programs have done an excellent job of identifying and cultivating partner schools and mentor teachers, this work can be done more effectively if the SCDE assists in various ways. An institution-wide policy is needed on how to approach schools for practicum placements, research sites, and other purposes and how to cooperate with other universities in the selection of partner schools. Of particular importance is the expression of recognition and thanks to principals and mentor teachers: these people feel more respected if the whole institution celebrates their contribution rather than just the cohort team. At the government level, SCDEs are in constant contact with departments and representatives over matters of policy, funding, research, and so on. These interactions should be constantly used to promote the image and further the goals of the preservice enterprise.

ESTABLISHING A MULTI-COHORT PRESERVICE STRUCTURE

An important early step, we believe, in extending the social constructivist approach within the institution is to create other preservice cohorts. This provides a basis for achieving the approach more widely within preservice and allows for mutual support and a united front toward the larger institution. Creating multiple cohorts typically requires the approval of the SCDE; however, if the cost is not significantly higher it is likely to be allowed as largely a preservice matter. Some compromises may have to be made initially, for example with respect to the type of participation of tenure-track faculty or arrangements with practicum schools. At the University of Utah, when the multi-cohort structure was instituted in the 1980s, some faculty objected that having student teachers clustered in a few partner schools meant losing "the use of several exemplary practitioners in particular subject areas" (Arends &

Winitzky, 1996, p. 547). Disagreements over this issue were so strong at the time that they had to be resolved by allowing some professors to opt out of the cohort arrangement.

Division of the preservice student body into multiple cohorts may be done in a number of ways. At the University of Sydney, every student in the MTeach year-group of 250 belongs to two small cohorts, one for exploring general curriculum issues and the other for gaining knowledge and skills in their teaching-subject(s); they are in these groups for much of their campus studies. The main cohort at Bank Street College is the "conference group" of 5 to 7 students, who meet weekly with their faculty advisor to discuss their practicum experiences and related theoretical issues. However, Bank Street also has a number of small, integrated programs with cohort features, such as the elementary preservice program we studied. At NYU there are only about 40 students in each of the third and fourth years of the elementary preservice undergraduate program, and these cohorts have their own faculty team, inte-grated programming, and a close community experience. All the teacher can-didates at Central Connecticut State University are assigned to cohort groups for purposes of "work[ing] collaboratively on projects that become part of their developmental portfolios" (Lemma, 1999, p. 186). This approach to pro-ject work is seen as "important for developing dispositions toward coopera-tion, collaboration, and collective inquiry" (p. 214).

Some universities with large numbers of preservice enrollees in a given year divide the students into cohorts for nearly all their studies, going well beyond the degree of cohort separation found in many of the programs noted above. As mentioned in Chapter 1, this is done in the fifth year of preservice education at the University of Utah (Arends & Winitzky, 1996; Bullough & Gitlin, 1995; Winitzky, Stoddart, & O'Keefe, 1992) and at Portland State University (Peterson et al., 1995). In the Utah program, candidates in the cohorts "take the same classes together [and] pursue field experiences together" (Winitzky, Stoddart, & O'Keefe, 1992, pp. 11–12). At Portland State the students in each cohort "take classes together, are grouped in field placements, experience retreats and team building activities, share a faculty team, and engage in reflection about their work" (Peterson et al., 1995, p. 30). Dagenais and Wideen (1999) state that at Simon Fraser University, "students work in cohort groups of 24 to 36 with two faculty associates [teachers on loan full-time from the school board] and one professor" (p. 171). These three faculty are responsible for "developing the program" for their cohort of student teachers (p. 174). The authors report that the "structural freedom and flexibility embedded at the program level allow teacher educators to create their own curriculum according to their interests and in response to their stu-dents" (p. 181).

At OISE/UT the 1-year post-baccalaureate elementary B.Ed. degree has a multi-cohort structure like that at Utah, Portland State, and Simon Fraser, although the cohorts are about twice the size (around 65) thus allowing for a larger faculty team. Each faculty team has two full-time coordinators and three or four part-time members (who may be full-time in the school of education, teaching in other programs as well). At present there are 9 elementary cohort programs, including our Mid-Town program. Applicants who have been accepted to the program attend an "Options Night" several months prior to the start of the academic year and choose their cohort based on presentations made by the faculty teams. Many students from the year just ending also go to Options Night and help advise the new candidates on their choice. The candidates attend three presentations and submit three rank-ordered choices; they are assigned to their first, second, or third choice on a first-come-first-served basis.

In what ways, if any, should multiple preservice cohort programs differ from one another, apart from being largely separate entities with different names? At most universities with this structure, each program has a somewhat distinctive emphasis while adhering to shared general principles and requirements. At Portland State, as indicated in chapter 1, although each cohort has its own thematic focus, a common program framework ensures competence in "planning, curriculum, instruction, pupil assessment, classroom management, teacher reflection, and professional development" (Peterson et al., 1995, p. 30). In Sydney's MTeach, at the secondary level, much of the cohort experience occurs in groups distinguished by their teaching-subject focus (for example, English, mathematics, or science). On the whole, we believe a subject focus is preferable to a thematic one at the secondary level, given the importance of subject areas to secondary teachers and their students. If general themes are dealt with in the context of secondary candidates' teaching subjects they become integrated into the subjects and so are more likely to be attended to when the new teachers enter the profession.

At the elementary level, some cohort differentiation along thematic lines helps faculty and students take ownership of their program and express their particular interests and talents. At OISE/UT, for example, one program emphasizes drama, another technology, another literacy, and another group-work (using the Tribes approach). However, we believe the bulk of each program should address issues of concern to all elementary teachers: the goals of schooling, approaches to literacy and math teaching, the arts, curriculum modification and integration, assessment and evaluation, community building, equity and inclusion, classroom management, teacher inquiry, and so on.

Much of the distinctiveness of a cohort program lies in the *manner* in which the goals of the program are pursued. Each faculty team can decide for itself to a large extent the nature and timing of its activities, thus modeling a constructivist approach to programming. This results in greater commitment, inventiveness, and satisfaction among faculty. As we saw earlier, at Simon Fraser it is considered important that each faculty team is free to develop the curriculum "according to their interests and in response to their students." Similarly, several OISE/UT program coordinators in a recent focus group meeting emphasized the value of cohort autonomy. Ivor commented: "We are not just in our big team, there are the individual [cohort] teams . . . and you develop your own knowledge and your own understanding through discussion and dialogue; and then you just do what you think is best." And John said he liked the fact that, after the coordinators meeting, you have

> the autonomy to go back and hash it out with your small team, and say what does this mean for us? For instance, Lynn and I . . . believe in critical thinking, there's no doubt about it, but we know that people don't think critically when they are in survival mode; so we pay attention [to our students], asking . . . do they have enough to get started next year, so that they think about what they are doing with the kids instead of just thinking about themselves. . . . So I like the autonomy. It means you're not under pressure to always follow a common idea.

BUILDING CONNECTIONS
BETWEEN COHORT PROGRAMS

The autonomy of cohort programs is a precious commodity and is a large reason for their ability to develop in a social constructivist direction. However, faculty teams can also learn from each other and support each other in a variety of ways. Although we know of several universities with multiple cohort programs, we are not very familiar with how the cohorts interact and collaborate. Accordingly, in illustrating strategies in this area we will again focus on our own institution.

One of the authors (Clare) helped establish the Mid-Town cohort program at OISE/UT in the late 1980s, coordinated and taught in it for several years, and then was director of the whole elementary division for three years (2000–2003) while continuing to teach in Mid-Town. (Clive joined the program on a halftime basis in 1995). The Mid-Town faculty team was the first to take full advantage of the cohort arrangement, which had existed at the elementary level since the early 1980s. We integrated the program, established an inquiry orientation for the students, and built community within the cohort. We also conducted research on the program and wrote about the Mid-Town approach in research reports and journal articles. This gave us a basis for sharing principles and practices with the other OISE/UT cohort programs and for helping them move in a similar direction.

When Clare became Director of Elementary Preservice in summer 2000, the coordinators were a loosely knit group lacking a strong sense of empowerment. Meetings tended to be called on an ad hoc basis to deal with particular matters, and much of the time was spent implementing directives rather than making decisions. Clare felt that the first priority was to build community in the group to strengthen morale and facilitate working together. Early in the first term she hosted a barbecue at her home for all elementary preservice instructors, administrators, and support staff; from then on, these events were held two or three times a year. Other less formal social gatherings took place on or near the campus. An email conference was established for the coordinators, with inviting messages posted every day; a second email folder was set up for sharing materials. At meetings of the group, Clare established a format that ensured a friendly atmosphere and much joking and laughter. Among other activities, coordinators were invited to take turns in opening each meeting with a brief reading, song, skit, or the like.

The coordinator meetings were scheduled regularly once a month at a time agreeable to all. Clare kept the coordinators fully informed about happenings in the institution and involved them in policy decisions on matters over which she had control. Coordinators sat on the hiring committees for new contract staff and helped choose the questions to be posed to candidates. The friendly atmosphere and the coordinators' growing knowledge of each other ensured collegial decision making and a sense of safety in sharing opinions and concerns. Subcommittees were formed to address particular issues, and reporting from these committees was an important part of the monthly agenda.

The practicum subcommittee was especially active. The committee realized early that a problem with the practicum was that not all faculty had a clear sense of how to supervise; accordingly, it decided to offer a workshop on supervision immediately preceding the first practicum session. This workshop was well attended by both new and experienced faculty, and included role-playing activities and discussion of expectations, procedures, and commonly asked questions. The committee now offers workshops on supervision before each practicum session, and continues to delve more deeply into the area. It has also prepared the invaluable document, *Guidelines for Practicum Supervision*, using the Mid-Town practicum handbook on this topic as a starting point.

As comfort levels rose, the coordinators began to share openly their concerns about a variety of matters. Supervision loads were unevenly distributed, with some faculty having minimal supervision and others an unmanageable amount. (In the OISE/UT model, the cohort teams do the supervision; we do not hire staff specifically for this role.) Clare and the coordinators worked with the associate dean to assign an equitable supervision load to each preservice faculty member, eventually producing a chart showing everyone's supervision allocation. A subcommittee chaired by Louise (the elementary practicum director, who was an integral part of the coordinator group) prepared guidelines for dealing with students experiencing harassment (sexual, racial, ethnic, etc.) in the practicum. John developed a revision of Mid-Town's formative evaluation form for the practicum, which each cohort faculty team then shaped to reflect its program's emphases. And Susan's work on lesson plan formats was widely shared and used among the cohorts.

The coordinator group identified as a key need the improvement of links with partner schools and, related to this, provision of professional development for the principals and mentor teachers in the schools. We also saw that such work could not be done adequately by cohort teams acting alone; accordingly, we sought to hold combined events. For example, we organized a breakfast for the principals of all our practicum schools (approximately 90 of the 120 principals attended), which included a talk by our then dean, Michael Fullan, on large-scale literacy reform. Another event for the approximately 800 mentor teachers included a keynote address on technology and literacy by David Booth, discussion of the mentor teacher role, and a publishers' display. Though done on a shoestring budget, both events involved all the cohort programs and were highly successful.

Another activity begun by the coordinator group was Math Activity Day (MAD). This is organized annually by a subcommittee that includes coordinators and mathematics instructors under the leadership of Lucy, coordinator of the Cross-town program, who is a specialist in the math area. To make linkages with local school districts and expose our cohorts to up-to-date expertise, the subcommittee invited school district mathematics consultants to give a range of workshops on math teaching. At each coordinators' meeting the logistics for the day were discussed; all the coordinators had to agree to "give up" a day in their regular program for MAD and commit to helping organize their cohorts. Despite a minimal budget, the day included a keynote speaker, a wide variety of workshops, and a publishers' display. Math Activity Day, now in its third year, is enshrined in elementary preservice and serves to increase expertise among instructors and student teachers and demonstrate our commitment to mathematics education.

One of the peculiarities of preservice at OISE/UT is the absence of a formal course on special education; as a result, attention to special education can vary widely from one cohort to another. For example, while Jackie, coordinator of the Doncrest program, had extensive background in special education and so was able to integrate it naturally into her program, other cohort teams did not have the required level of expertise. To help ameliorate the problem, the elementary educational psychology instructors (some of whom are coordinators) formed a subcommittee and focused their efforts initially on special education. They became involved in a range of activities. For example, Lucy and Hazel conducted formal focus groups with faculty, students, and graduates of the program to study the needs of beginning teachers regarding special education. Kathy and Jackie took the lead in putting together a packet of readings on special education to be used in all cohorts. They also developed a glossary of terms and practice exercises to help students prepare for the teacher certification test in this area. This subcommittee has had tremendous impact on elementary preservice, with the general level of instruction for special education improving significantly.

One of the great breakthroughs of the coordinator group was to begin systematic research on the cohort programs, similar to that conducted in Mid-Town over the years. This was aided in part by "mini-grants" made available to preservice instructors by the dean's office. Because this was a new scheme, Clare encouraged the coordinators and other instructors to apply, and worked closely with them to help them succeed in the competition. The coordinator group as a whole also began to conduct research on certain matters of interest to all the programs. For example, many participated in a study of the preservice admissions process, and all collaborated in a research project on assignments. We will describe both these projects in detail in the next chapter.

DEVELOPING PRINCIPLES, STRUCTURES, AND RELATIONSHIPS IN THE INSTITUTION

Establishing collaboration and mutual support among cohort programs is a major step forward and helps increase their effectiveness and viability. However, as discussed earlier, the values, attitudes, and level of support in the institution as a whole are also very important for the preservice enterprise. We will now look at what can be done at this wider level.

Institutional philosophy and approach. In order to influence the larger institution toward a social constructivist approach and toward greater support of preservice, we need to develop a coherent conception that we can share in the SCDE and try to have implemented in a systematic fashion. As far as possible, that conception should be developed *with* others in the institution. Fortunately, most SCDEs in countries with a tradition of progressive educational theory are officially committed to a constructivist, communal, inclusive philosophy, and we can take advantage of this in seeking to spread a social constructivist approach. However, we need a more detailed articulation of what this means than is commonly available. Just as teachers and teacher educators who say they believe in constructivism often have difficulty explaining what it is, so education administrators and faculty in general tend to be unclear about the precise implications of this stance.

The basic principles of a social constructivist approach to education, as we understand it, were elaborated in earlier chapters. They include the agency of learners in constructing their own knowledge and way of life; the need for close links between experience, practice, and theory; and the importance of community and inclusion in teaching and learning. When these and related principles are applied to the institutional setting, they have many implications that we believe the whole SCDE should embrace, including the following:

(i) the necessity of a student-centered approach to teaching, teacher education, and education studies generally; (ii) the central importance of practitioners and practice-oriented scholars such as teachers and teacher educators; (iii) the need for practitioners, practice-oriented faculty, and more abstract theorists to work closely together; and (iv) the need for community, democracy, and mutual respect in the institution.

Moving to a more practical level, the aforementioned position has many structural and policy implications for SCDEs and universities. For example, preservice faculty should be supported, rewarded, and celebrated to the same degree as non-preservice faculty. Preservice faculty should have a major say in policy and hiring decisions throughout the institution. The preservice function should receive a large proportion of the revenue it earns and have significant control over its budget. And SCDE representatives should advocate strongly for the preservice function in settings beyond the SCDE such as the university at large, school boards, and governments.

How can we go about elaborating and disseminating such a philosophy and practical approach in our SCDE? By way of illustration, some of the actions taken at OISE/UT include the following. A group of us in preservice have begun to develop a systematic position of this kind and are sharing it through our writings. The coordinator group, as described earlier, has developed many of the practical details. Several of us engage in joint research and writing on relevant topics with faculty who are not involved—or only partly involved—in preservice. Preservice faculty serve on general SCDE committees where relevant ideas and policies are discussed. And elementary preservice offers a series of research seminars to share the findings of their research on preservice education and related concepts and implications.

A significant new development in this direction occurred at OISE/UT over the past year. Several of us participated in the organization of a 1-day, in-house symposium on "teaching for depth," both in general and in teacher education. This is a topic we view as central to social constructivism since "teaching for understanding," as it is often called, requires that learners be interested in and engaged by their learning and relate it to their previous ideas, past experience, and life beyond the school. Planning for the symposium took place over 8 months and involved sharing papers and engaging in intense conceptual discussion with faculty from the Institute of Child Study and the Center for Cognitive Science who were on the planning committee, including Carl Bereiter, a prominent academic in the cognitive science field.

On the day itself, general sessions on the symposium theme were held in the morning, and in the afternoon 13 of our preservice staff—elementary and secondary, contract and tenure-track—led workshops dealing with their understanding of teaching for depth and how they implement it in their preservice program. After the symposium, the workshop leaders were asked to submit brief summaries of their ideas and practices and a small group of us used these as a basis for formulating criteria of teaching for depth and ways to support such teaching in preservice education. These formulations were then shared with all the cohort coordinators and other leaders in the school of education.

While not a large proportion of non-preservice faculty were involved in the symposium and follow-up, we feel we are on a path to articulating a set of ideas on preservice education and sharing them with other parts of the institution. We plan in future to have more such sessions where we simultaneously explore basic issues in education and directions for preservice education. For example, next year an international conference on teacher education will be held at OISE/UT and a major strand of the conference will be ongoing discussion of the ideas developed in the symposium and its follow-up activities.

Administrative policies, structures, and practices. Apart from developing and disseminating a philosophy and approach in the institution, many practical details need to be worked through that may not be of interest to everyone but are crucial for the success of the preservice enterprise. These also need to be explicitly formulated so they are not implemented in an accidental and ad hoc manner. Initially, many of them will be negotiated and developed in the course of everyday institutional management; accordingly, it is important to appoint suitable administrators from the beginning. Policy development cannot be separated from the appointment process, because once an inappropriate appointment has been made to a key position, sound policy development will be continually subverted; or, more positively, the term of a good administrator will be marked by sound policy development on a wide range of matters.

The associate dean or program director ultimately responsible for preservice, then, should be someone who is knowledgeable about preservice education and committed to the general philosophy and approach outlined previously. And other key preservice administrators need to be people who are able to give leadership in the same general direction, foster connections, and provide organizational support while allowing the cohort teams a considerable degree of autonomy and ownership. To help ensure appointments of these kinds, preservice representatives must have a major role in the appointment process.

In order to promote the cause of preservice, the associate dean or other senior administrator should have substantial power in the dean's office. In turn, however, he or she should allow a considerable degree of power to preservice administrators and instructional staff. As Tom (1997) has pointed out, associate deans are typically too far removed from the work of preservice to micromanage. This is especially so where there are multiple cohort programs rather than just a couple of general programs taken by large numbers of students. Hiring of contract preservice faculty, for example, must be largely in the hands of the cohort programs so they can hire people they actually need and who they know will be competent. Similarly, preservice administrators and faculty should have a major role in the hiring of tenure-track faculty who will teach in preservice, and in the appointment of tenure-track faculty to particular cohort teams. Further, the preservice function must have control over the practicum office so they can ensure that it is indeed a help in the placement process: too often cohort teams have to work around the practicum office, or just do the job themselves to make sure it is done well.

A key structural issue is the nature of the relationship between the preservice enterprise and specialized academic departments, centers, and programs. At OISE/UT we have a "matrix" structure, according to which each of the 5 specialist departments supplies tenure-track faculty to preservice and houses some of the contract preservice faculty. This does not work very well at present: preservice has very limited administrative space and presence, and contract preservice faculty are scattered around the building with little sense of having a home. Equally, tenure-track faculty involved in preservice have no obvious place to meet up with other preservice staff, which tends to reinforce their primary affiliation to their academic department. On the other hand, however, even if there was a "department" of preservice education we do not think many tenure-track faculty, ourselves included, would want to be housed in it because that would separate us even more from the departments. Tom (1997) discusses at length these kinds of dilemmas and in the end recommends certain principles that should be followed, regardless of the precise structure; and that is what we would advocate. Whether there should be a matrix structure, a separate department of teacher education, or some other arrangement is hard to judge, though we should continue to pursue this question. What matters most, however, is implementation of *policies and practices* that ensure that preservice administrators have suitable facilities; contract preservice faculty have an appropriate home base and adequate support; abundant opportunities exist for tenure-track and contract faculty to mingle and work together in an attractive setting; and preservice administrators and faculty have sufficient control over hiring, appointments, budgeting, and other matters to run a strong program. Unfortunately, however, it is rare to find SCDEs in which such policies and practices are consistently followed.

Speaking of budget, this of course has long been a sore point in teacher education. Tom (1997) describes a school of education in which, "even though teacher education generated about three-quarters of the school of education's tuition income, such programming received less than half of that income and often was reduced to being little more than a source of financial aid for doctoral students" (p. 204). Speaking generally, he observes that "teacher education does tend to subsidize graduate instruction within the education unit" (p. 204). Of course, given the value of the specialist disciplines to preservice education, which Tom acknowledges, it is difficult to determine precisely how much of the revenue should go to the preservice function. However, in our view, the proportion at present is usually far too low, reflecting the second-class status of preservice education that we believe SCDEs should firmly reject. And not only should the funding be larger, but much of it should be allocated directly to the preservice function so it can be spent appropriately.

Among the urgent needs that increased funding would allow us to meet are the following: a more equitable workload for preservice faculty; more adequate space and facilities for preservice; funding to help contract faculty conduct research and attend professional workshops and conferences; release time for mentor teachers so they can engage in professional development and teacher research; more adequate remuneration for practicum supervisors and mentor teachers (or their schools); and regular events for mentor teachers and principals of partner schools to recognize their contribution to preservice education. Many of these are not big ticket items; some, as we have indicated, can be done "on a shoestring." However, the fact that we have to do them on a shoestring, or not at all, is symptomatic of the problem. And the symbolism of this situation is not lost on school personnel, teacher educators, student teachers, or young tenure-track professors of education.

Beyond structural and budgetary issues, a number of more specific matters need attention. We have already mentioned the key importance of involving preservice staff in the hiring and appointments process, and explicit policies to ensure this should be developed. Admissions is another area in need of adequate funding, policy development, and implementation. Admitting candidates who clearly are unsuited to teaching has a very harmful impact on the program, not to mention on the teaching profession in the future. Even the admission of graduate students should be considered in relation to the needs of preservice. At Stanford, many doctoral applicants are selected in part because of their suitability for preservice teaching and supervision, and this is a significant factor in the strength of the preservice program. Another key matter is space. We have stressed the need for appropriate administrative and faculty space, but it is just as important to have attractive classroom space that is large enough and flexible enough to accommodate the cohort programs in their various configurations. As discussed in chapter 4, this is enormously important for good teaching and community development.

Faculty workload and reward levels are also crucial; they should be comparable with those for other types of work in the SCDE. If participation in preservice teaching requires a sacrifice on the part of tenure-track faculty, few of them will engage in it to a significant degree, given the current lower status of such work. Dagenais and Wideen (1999) suggest that tenure considerations for the professorship be expanded, with greater recognition "given to initiatives in program development as valuable contributions to the discipline." This may encourage tenure-track faculty to become more involved in teacher education, thus giving them "a more profound understanding and appreciation of the culture of the schools from which the faculty associates come and into which the students must integrate" (p. 181). With respect to contract faculty, again their workload and remuneration must reflect the great importance and demanding nature of preservice teaching and supervision. Also, such faculty should be incorporated into the life of the institution to a greater extent than at present. Dagenais and Wideen (1999), on the basis of their study of the Simon Fraser preservice program, propose that "faculty associate membership in the university community could be substantially expanded to include participation in decision-making forums such as faculty meetings and hiring committees for all faculty positions" (p. 181). A particular issue is the length of term of contract faculty on loan from school boards. Again, Dagenais and Wideen (1999) recommend that "terms of residence in the faculty could be modified for faculty associates who have initiated program innovations and wish to be involved in the continuation of these projects" (p. 181). Too often strict rules are applied to limited-term appointments, resulting in losing outstanding faculty at the peak of their contribution to the program.

In many of these matters it will be necessary to make compromises from time to time, as the University of Utah case illustrated. For example, it may be necessary to exempt some tenure-stream faculty from preservice teaching who are not suited to the role or simply not interested in it. Sometimes tenure-track faculty or doctoral students not entirely suited to preservice may have to be included on a cohort team for practical reasons. And not all tenure-stream preservice instructors may be required to do practicum supervision, even though that would be ideal. However, through all the juggling and negotiation, it should be clear that the preservice enterprise is on an equal footing with other units and programs in the institution, that a great deal of consultation is taking place, and that there is a commitment to increasing the support for preservice over time. Above all, there must be transparency in decisions: on budget, hiring, faculty offices, and so on. People must be able to see the what, how, and why of the actions taken, even where they disagree with the outcome. Only in this way will they have confidence that the institution is doing its utmost for preservice and that things will improve as better solutions are developed.

Relationships in the institution.   Favorable administrative policies and arrangements will take us a considerable distance, but in addition, a lot of relationship building with units and individuals can be done directly by the preservice enterprise. The social dimension is important here. At OISE/UT, for example, we invite members of academic and administrative units to our main preservice social gatherings and try as far as possible to get to know them as individuals. In doing so, we make a point of including junior as well as senior administrative staff members.

The specialist academic departments are of course a key arena for relationship building. We noted earlier some of the information activities that can be carried out, and the value of engaging in joint teaching, supervision, research, and writing with specialist education faculty beyond the preservice function. We also need to involve tenure-track faculty from the departments in preservice activities as much as possible so they can see what we do and why. When doing so, we need to work closely with individual faculty to find out what kind of involvement is best for them. The physical set-up can be very important here. For example, we arranged to have the coordinators of two elementary cohort programs housed in the Center for Teacher Development (within the Curriculum, Teaching, and Learning Department), where they come in frequent contact with tenure-track faculty who have an interest in teacher education.

It is also important to establish connections with various administrative offices in the SCDE. For example, at OISE/UT we have developed a close relationship with the research office, explaining the type of research we do and seeking the advice of the associate dean (research) on how to refine research proposals so they are more likely to be funded. In a recent multiyear study of inservice teacher education, we had to obtain two successive 1-year extensions of the project because of problems both within the research team and at the school board level. In the end, for a variety of reasons, it was not possible to conduct the research. Throughout this difficult experience, the associate dean of research served as a supportive mediator and gave us advice on how to keep intact our good relationship with the school board and funding agency.

A positive relationship with the registrar's office has also served us well over the years. Since the 1996 merger of the preservice and graduate functions at OISE/UT, we have been fortunate to have an outstanding registrar who is not only a strong administrator but also humane toward students and sympathetic to our approach to preservice education. We have worked closely with her and her colleagues on admissions and have together been able to develop a process that is relatively enjoyable for the faculty and yields a high proportion of strong preservice students. She has supported us well, showing understanding and flexibility as we deal with difficult hard-luck cases, failing students who should fail, complex student appeals, and so on. As discussed elsewhere, the registrar and her staff have been especially helpful in facilitating our research on the admissions process. All these benefits are due largely to the personal qualities of the registrar but partly to our work in developing general understandings with her and explaining in detail the nature of each issue and case.

Several other administrative offices are of significance for preservice programming. We have worked closely with the finance officers at both the departmental and school of education level to resolve thorny issues such as what funds can be carried over from one year to the next, sources of funding for printing and photocopying, and how to recoup copying expenses from students. The student services office has been very supportive in dealing with students with health problems or students who are harassing faculty or fellow students. The human resources office is also important for a variety of staffing issues; and the space management office is a key one to cultivate, given the significance of space for cohort programs.

These then are a range of general and specific strategies we can use in attempting to create a more sympathetic and supportive environment for our social constructivist preservice program. As we have said, this is a daunting task given all our other responsibilities. We do not wish to downplay the amount of work involved or exaggerate the chances of being successful. However, such activity is potentially interesting and fulfilling and we can learn a great deal from it; and the more we can do along these lines, the more the work in our own program will be facilitated and enhanced.

CHAPTER 7

Researching the Program

[W]e teachers bring a depth of awareness to our data that outside researchers cannot begin to match.

> —Ruth Hubbard and Brenda Power,
> *The Art of Classroom Inquiry*

As noted in chapter 1, in his 1998 AERA vice presidential address, Ken Zeichner stated that "more and more of the research about teacher education is being conducted by those who actually do the work of teacher education." Further, he described this as a very salutary trend; "the birth of the self-study in teacher education movement around 1990 has been probably the single most significant development ever in the field of teacher education research" (Zeichner, 1998, p. 19). Why is "self-study" research on preservice practice so important? According to Zeichner, such research is useful in part because it enables us to critique and improve our program. For example, in recent times research of this kind has "exposed gaps between what [teacher educators] thought they were doing and how their students experienced their teaching" (p. 40). In addition, self-study research is valuable because it is carried out by people who are "sensitive to the personal and social complexities" of teacher education (p. 41). Accordingly, it can often be more effective than "arm's length" research.

In this chapter we will begin by discussing these and other reasons for researching one's preservice program. We will then go on to look at possible topics and levels of self-study research; suitable research methodology; and how some of the challenges of research on one's own program can be overcome. To illustrate the various issues we will once again draw on our experience at OISE/UT.

WHY RESEARCH ONE'S OWN PRESERVICE PROGRAM?

As discussed in the previous chapter, conducting research on our own program is important to gain support for preservice education within our institution and to show non-preservice colleagues that we are serious about research. It helps shore up our position in the SCDE and university, where increasingly a strong research record is required of preservice educators (Goodlad, 1990b; Tom, 1997); and it enables us to engage in discussions about research with non-preservice faculty. It also means we can participate more effectively in teaching graduate courses on research and supervising graduate students. For example, at OISE/UT the authors teach the graduate course Thoughtful Teaching and Practitioner Inquiry, taken each year by about 20 master's and doctoral students; this course explores the rationale for teacher research and requires each student to do a small research project in their own classroom or jointly with a practicing teacher or teacher educator in *their* classroom. As well as providing readings on research methodology, we are able to share with the students our own strategies and experiences of research planning, data gathering, data analysis, and report writing. As the students go on to conduct research for their degree (which may build in part on the research done for the course), they find this early interaction with researchers helpful, and they often call on one of us to serve as their thesis supervisor.

Researching one's own preservice program is also a sound idea because it is relatively feasible. As we will describe later, a few years ago Clare was strongly advised by the chair of her departmental research committee to do her research in another program, on the grounds that such research would better fit the accepted norms of scholarly inquiry. However, she resisted on grounds of practicality (among others) and ultimately was supported in this. Preservice teacher education, especially on the model we are following, is so time consuming that if we are to do much research it has to be largely in the context of our own program. We already know a great deal about the program, the students, our colleagues, and the partner schools, and so have much of the necessary background information needed. Also, less time is required to explain the nature of the research, gain the consent of those participating, and conduct surveys, interviews, and the like. The time factor is noted by Tom (1997) when he comments:

> My own way of coping with the extraordinary amount of time needed to do good scholarship, as well as first-rate clinical work, is to inquire into my clinical work. . . . I made this decision in order to survive professionally. If I did not combine scholarship and clinical work, one or the other had to be short-changed. (p. 30)

Another reason for doing self-study research on one's preservice practice, of course, is to provide a basis for improving it: for example, to expose the "gaps" between what we are doing and how our students experience what we are doing, as Zeichner (1998) put it. This involves actually asking our students about their experience of the program, something that is done remarkably seldom apart from brief course evaluations. Improvement of practice cannot be achieved simply by applying the research conducted by others. As discussed in chapter 1, the fruits of other people's research is usually too abstract as it stands. While it can point us in a broad direction, we have to figure out the details of a sound program for our students. Teacher educators, like all teachers, must be researchers, observing in their classroom, modifying the curriculum to fit their diverse students, and assessing the effects of these modifications.

The following example illustrates how research has had an impact on our program. In a follow-up study of 11 of our Mid-Town graduates 2 years after completing the program, we found they had a number of concerns about their initial readiness for literacy teaching. While they were generally pleased with our literacy course, some felt it should have prepared them better for the "nitty-gritty" of literacy teaching and in particular for starting up the program in the first year. One graduate said:

> At the beginning you just want answers. You don't want someone to say "What are we going to do?" because you don't know what to do. At the beginning it's better if somebody tells you how to do it, and then once you get comfortable with that you can modify it on your own.

In light of our findings from this study we took a number of steps. We contacted supervisory officers in the school districts to find ways to link the teacher education program more fully with the school district programs, and arranged for local school literacy coordinators to do workshops for our student teachers on school district initiatives such as the Early Years Literacy Program, Reading Recovery, and the Diagnostic Reading Assessment. In their practice teaching schools, students are now required to seek out the literacy coordinator and shadow him or her for half a day to learn about school district programs and become familiar with the curriculum materials they will be expected to use. We encourage our students to do their final internship in one of the Early Years Literacy Program schools, and when they do this we arrange for the internship to be supervised by the literacy coordinator in the school, with special emphasis on how to start up your literacy program. We give our students more specific and direct information than in the past about literacy teaching and offer optional workshops on getting started in September. We make available to them packages of literacy activities they could use in September (e.g., poetry activities, 100 activities to do with a novel study, and so on). All this, despite the fact that we still believe the main focus should be on helping students acquire a broad *approach* to literacy teaching rather than a "bag of tricks." However, we have found that providing them with concrete help in the aforementioned ways reduces their anxiety about the first year of teaching and does not necessarily reduce their grasp of more general principles (though one must always be on guard against reinforcing a how-to mentality).

A key reason for doing self-study research is to *model* for our student teachers a reflective approach to teaching. As Zeichner (1998) has said, "[t]his disciplined and systematic inquiry into one's own teaching practice . . . provides a model for prospective teachers and teachers of the kind of inquiry that more and more teacher educators are hoping their students employ" (p. 41). Research on our preservice practice, then, is not just a nice extra; it goes to the heart of effective teaching. Student teachers have to learn how to do research in the classroom, how to observe, modify, individualize, and assess; and much of this they can learn through our example. But just as importantly, if we do not practice it ourselves the students may well dismiss our advocacy of teacher research as merely an academic fad.

Someone might accept all the above arguments for doing self-study inquiry in preservice education but still ask: Why call it "research"? The main reason for doing so is because it *is* research, it is systematic inquiry into key matters; and to deny this is to buy into a whole paradigm with which social constructivists disagree. Furthermore, such a stance has important consequences for the status, reward, and support of teacher educators within the SCDE and beyond. According to Schön (1983), reflective practitioners are to be seen as "researchers" and "experimenters" (pp. 66–69), as generators of *theory*, with nonpractitioner university researchers largely in a dependent role. And viewing inquiry into one's practice in these terms has "implications for the professional's relation to . . . clients, for the organizational settings of practice, for the future interaction of research and practice, and for the place of the professions in the larger society" (p. ix). Speaking of teachers in general, Cochran-Smith and Lytle (1993) point to the absurdity of a situation where teachers, throughout their careers, "are expected to learn about their own profession not by studying their own experiences but by studying the findings of those who are not themselves school-based teachers" (p. 1). Applying these insights specifically to teachers of teachers, we see the need to take seriously their role as the key researchers on preservice education.

SELECTING TOPICS AND LEVELS FOR RESEARCH

What kinds of topics are suitable for research on our program? A key principle is to narrow down the topic to a particular problem or area so it is manageable; we should not try to do too much at once. As Hubbard and Power (1993) say, "[t]he more specific you are, the easier it will be to develop research procedures" (p. 7); further, the easier it is to locate relevant research literature. We should not feel guilty about narrowing our focus in this way, because a narrow topic may still have quite broad implications, given the interconnectedness of educational phenomena. For example, a study of student teachers' experience of assignments may lead to major insights into fragmentation in the program, lack of connection between theory and practice, and an overly prescriptive pedagogy on the part of the faculty.

Another important principle of selection is to begin with research issues that are close at hand and of immediate interest. Teacher research must be something we do gladly, otherwise we will not normally do it, given all the other pressures we are under. Hubbard and Power (1993) speak of investigating "what intrigues you in your classroom, what you wonder about" (p. 6). This gives us added motivation and positions us well to do effective research. For example, when we first began researching our program, a major preoccupation of ours was increasing the inquiry aspect of the program and specifically the action research component. Accordingly, we did several studies on the action research process, its impact on the student teachers, its impact on ourselves, how to make it more effective, and how our graduates felt about it after a year of teaching. At another point, the issue of adding an internship to our program arose, something we were opposed to at the time; so we conducted research on the internship in the first year of its implementation, and the research changed our minds somewhat. Similarly, we decided to do a study of our preservice admissions process at a time when there was talk of dismantling it to reduce costs. The research revealed some needed changes but also many strengths in the existing process, thus slowing the momentum of the proposed modifications.

A third principle of topic selection is to move gradually toward more comprehensive research on our program. We should begin to explore connections between various research areas, for example between the university campus program and the practicum, or between the campus program and the cohort community. This deepens our analysis, gives greater direction to the program, and enables us to justify the program more broadly to others. It also provides us with a "research program," which is often viewed as essential in a research-intensive university. In our own research we have moved, roughly speaking, from a focus on action research to study of the cohort community, to inquiry into the campus program, to exploring links between the campus program and the practicum, to studying the characteristics of a good practicum placement and what student teachers learn in the practicum, to examining the situation of contract faculty in preservice education, and now to follow-up studies of the impact of the preservice program on our graduates' approach to teaching, especially in literacy education. However, other preservice educators may take quite a different path to a comprehensive research program.

Although studying one's own program is the essential starting point and main ongoing focus of self-study research, we should as far as possible do research at other levels of preservice practice as well, in collaboration with others. The most obvious next level is joint study with other cohort teams. This is perhaps the most enjoyable type of extended research and the one with the most payoff in terms of understanding one's own program. Earlier we spoke of collaborative research by the coordinator group at OISE/UT. We present here an example of this research to show how a study can cut across cohort programs.

Research across the cohort programs. Problems with respect to assignments surfaced in the Mid-Town program several years ago: student morale was being adversely affected by "bunching" of assignments at particular times of the year, duplication of assigned tasks, requiring assignments during the practicum, and simply an excessive assignment load. The Mid-Town team surveyed and interviewed the students on the problem and achieved some success in overcoming it. However, a couple of years into her term as director of elementary preservice, Clare felt it would be useful to explore the area across all the cohorts. Accordingly, she suggested to the group that a major initiative for the coordinators for the 2002–2003 academic year be a self-study of our assignments. The suggestion was well received and, over the year, a significant proportion of each monthly meeting was devoted to this research. We worked through a five-step process:

> Session 1—Working in small groups (4–6 coordinators) we all addressed the question, Why do you require students to complete assignments?
>
> Session 2—Each group addressed a distinct question, for example, How do you know when an assignment is not working?
>
> Session 3—As a whole group we decided on a research methodology (survey rather than individual interviews) and a specific focus (the structure of assignments). We generated specific questions or categories to be investigated.
>
> Session 4—As a group we reviewed and modified the questions. In addition, each pair of Coordinators tailored one part of the survey to assignments specific to their cohort.
>
> Session 5—Each pair of coordinators brought the tabulated data to a meeting where we talked about our findings.
>
> The instrument we developed had 45 questions (including 9 open-ended questions). The categories were: background information, coursework, feedback, practicum, and other comments. Questions included:

- To what extent was each of the following assignments effective/valuable in preparing you to be a teaching professional? (Each assignment for the particular cohort was listed.)

- To what extent should there be a self-evaluation component to all assignments?

- To what extent did your assignments help you to be successful in the practicum/internship?

- To what extent do you like assignments interconnecting across courses?

- To what extent is it important to you that you have a choice in topic for assignments?
- What motivates you to work diligently/fully on an assignment?
- What advice would you give your instructors regarding assignments?

Throughout the process there was lively discussion about the goals of the program and strategies for developing assignments. Because of the strong sense of community among the coordinators and the high trust level, the discussion was extremely honest. When analyzing and discussing the findings, some described responses that surprised and even upset them. However, there was no denying, sugarcoating, or blaming, only genuine inquiry into the effectiveness of our assignments. After our general meeting, each pair of coordinators took their individual cohort results to their faculty team for use in program development for the 2003–2004 academic year. Two further benefits of the collaborative research were that it allowed us to take some of our coordinators who are novice researchers through an entire research cycle, and it actualized our program principle of using research to inform our practice.

Research beyond the cohorts and the institution. The example just discussed is of research at the elementary education level. We have also done research at a preservice-wide level at OISE/UT: the internship and admissions studies noted earlier. In both these cases, several coordinators and others were involved in the research and we addressed the concerns of elementary and secondary education. However, we linked both studies back to our own program, looking at findings that were of particular interest to us and that helped throw light on how we could improve our program. For example, we considered how we could better prepare Mid-Town students to make the most of the internship, and examined the challenges that particular struggling or failing students had created in Mid-Town and how these might be addressed in the future.

It is also important to extend research beyond our SCDE to the extent feasible, while continuing to connect it to our own program. We did this in 2001–2002 in a study of preservice work in 7 Ontario universities, with special reference to how they were dealing with recent changes in the provincial school curriculum. Learning what others were doing in their literacy and math programs, in particular, suggested a number of ways of refining our courses in these areas. Further, we are now involved in a 3-year study of the preparation of elementary teacher candidates to teach literacy, studying programs at OISE/UT and 2 other universities: the University of Alberta in Edmonton, Alberta and Lakehead University in Ontario. Some of the OISE/UT students studied in the project are from Mid-Town, but many are not. This investigation is giving us a chance to relate our literacy teacher preparation work not only to approaches in other cohort programs at OISE/UT but also to those employed at other Canadian universities.

This last study represents a move to a level of preservice research to which not enough attention has been paid so far: follow-up study of new teacher graduates. In a report of a study that also examined the literacy teaching of recent graduates, Grossman, Valencia, Evans, Thompson, Martin, and Place (2000) observe that "most [teacher education] research stops with student teaching," and they stress the need to "follow teachers into the first year of teaching (and beyond)" (p. 632). Research of this type is important in raising the credibility of claims about the effectiveness of our preservice programs; perhaps we should have been doing more such research all along. However, as we have said before, it is important not to be too ambitious in self-study research, especially in the early stages.

CHOOSING APPROPRIATE RESEARCH METHODOLOGY

General research approach. The kind of self-study research we envisage for preservice educators is largely practice-based. This does not mean it cannot yield theory: on the contrary, a practice context for research is usually—some would say always—necessary for developing sound theory in the sociocultural domain (Carr, 1995; Cochran-Smith & Lytle, 2001; Noffke, 1997). However, one of its central goals is improvement of practice, and accordingly, much (though not all) of the research must be "qualitative" in nature, that is, it must deal with small samples and explore in depth what is happening in a given program or institution and how this can be enhanced.

Such inquiry is both a form of action research (Carr & Kemmis, 1986; Elliott, 1991, 1997; Noffke, 1997) and a type of grounded theory research (Punch, 1998; Strauss & Corbin, 1998). As such it involves *cycles* of observation, idea formation, program modification, and then further observation, assessment, reconceptualization, and so on. However, we wish to note that, in our experience, completing more than one cycle of *formal* research on a particular topic is often not feasible: subsequent cycles frequently have to be done informally as time pressure requires us to turn to other aspects of the program. We say this because, again, we should not attempt too much in our inquiry, with full-blown research at every phase; this will lead quickly to burnout or neglect of our practice.

Another qualification we would make with regard to research approach is that, while we largely agree with the grounded theory conception, we do not accept the suggestion that one should come to a research situation with an entirely open mind. Again, in our experience one always brings a great many understandings to a topic of research; and from a social constructivist perspective, that is as it should be, since new knowledge is created by building on prior knowledge and experience. We must have faith in ourselves, both that our previous ideas had some merit and that we will modify them in light of our research rather than clinging to them irrationally. One important feature of researching our own program is that we have built-in motivation to change unsound ideas because, unlike outside researchers, we have to live with the consequences. This is a point often overlooked by those who argue that arm's length research is more likely to lead to clear, objective insight.

Although a study employing a small number of in-depth interviews is usually viewed as qualitative research, we have found that the *quantities* in the data of such a study do influence our conclusions; and in fact journal reviewers usually want to know the response frequencies. Accordingly, even in a study of a small group of student teachers, preservice faculty, or mentor teachers it is important to determine and report how many of them thought a certain way on a given matter. In order to do this, we have to pursue many of the same issues with all the interviewees, while also of course exploring some individual or minority concerns.

Specific methods. Turning to particular self-study inquiry methods, we would recommend a strong emphasis on interviews and focus group discussions (tape-recorded and later transcribed); in our experience, they tend to yield the richest data. Surveys are valuable in pursuing certain types of questions, such as what proportion of students find a particular assignment useful (or not) or feel supported (or not) in the practicum. They also have the advantage that, if suitably formatted, they can be machine-read and the data quickly analyzed in a great many ways. However, we find that only a small proportion of the questions we are interested in can be investigated through surveys. The closed, check-off questions in a survey have to be too narrow, and one is often not sure what a response means or why it was given (whereas in an interview one can simply ask). Another limitation of surveys is that people typically do not enjoy completing them, especially open-ended questions that involve a significant amount of writing. Accordingly, the response rate on the latter type of question is often low, and it is difficult to assess whether this was due to the substance of the question or the non-engaging nature of the process. By contrast, we have found that people like the more personal nature of the interview or focus group situation and feel honored that their opinion is being sought in this intimate way. Interviews take time, of course; but equally, creating and formatting a good survey is time-consuming. Nevertheless, surveys definitely have at least a supplementary role in many studies.

The combining of interview and survey research (and also qualitative and quantitative methods) is illustrated by our study of preservice education in Ontario mentioned earlier. We surveyed a total of 47 teacher educators from 7 different universities, all of whom were specialists in either literacy or mathematics preservice instruction. We then interviewed 8 of them, 4 each at the elementary and secondary levels and 4 each in literacy and mathematics education; there was also a mix of women and men and variety in type of university, whether large or small, urban or rural. Most of the survey items were closed and machine-readable; as a result we were quickly able to generate over 200 pages of tables from these items, complete with tests of significance. The responses to the open survey questions required considerable interpretation and so we had to tabulate them by hand, but they also produced quantitative data. However, although we had all this quantitative material, in writing up the report only a small proportion of the findings came from this source, the rest being generated by our analysis of the 8 interview transcripts.

Because self-study research often has to be done with minimal funding, cost is an important consideration. Surveys are not necessarily expensive, but they can become so in terms of technical support if one makes them more comprehensive and machine-readable and seeks to analyze the responses in detail. In the case of interviews conducted by oneself (which we would recommend for small samples), the main cost item is transcribing the tapes. We have found that tape transcription is best done by specialists. For most teacher educators, transcribing is a tedious process and can reduce the motivation to do research; it is also very time-consuming, especially for a nonspecialist, and our time is better spent analyzing transcripts rather than producing them. In terms of research support from the SCDE, funding for transcribing is in our view a very high priority.

There are of course many other means of data gathering. Collection of documents (course outlines, bibliographies, lesson plans, etc.) is important and may not be expensive, depending on the form of the material. Student teacher portfolios are an increasingly popular type of data, although they can be difficult to copy and store. Student teacher journals are a rich source of data and are relatively convenient to collect. We have found that journaling by students usually works best if it is rather structured and done in the context of close interaction with faculty or fellow students or both. In general, in self-study research one should as far as possible use data already in existence (such as essays, action research reports, grades, etc.) in order to reduce the time, effort, and cost involved. Hubbard and Power (1993) observe that "research strategies can fit into your classroom routines" and "many of the records you keep as part of . . . evaluative strategies may be useful without any revision" (pp. 9, 12).

Finally, we would stress the importance of collaboration in research on one's own program. There is simply too much for one person to do, even over a 4- or 5-year period, and different researchers can complement each other's talents and interests and so work more effectively. Joint research can also be more enjoyable and can deepen the sense of community within the faculty team. Furthermore, such research provides students in the program with important modeling of teacher collaboration.

OVERCOMING THE CHALLENGES
OF SELF-STUDY RESEARCH

Despite all the advantages of self-study research on one's preservice program, it faces two somewhat related challenges: (i) relative difficulty in gaining institutional approval and funding, and (ii) relative lack of respect and reward in the academy. With regard to the first issue, we present here two stories from our own experience. The events described occurred several years ago, and the situation at our institution has improved significantly since then. However, we believe they illustrate a problem that persists to some degree to the present day for us and may still be a major concern at other universities. Also, the progress we have made has been hard won, and such battles may still be in the future for some preservice educators; they need to be aware of the potential difficulties.

Story #1. In the early stage of our research on the Mid-Town program, Clare attempted to get small-scale departmental funding for a study of student teachers' expectations of preservice education. This had become an issue in the action research work, because students tended to want to be *told* how to teach, and so the activity of conducting research on their teaching went against their initial expectations for the program. Clare's request for funding was denied by the departmental research committee, even though at the time small-scale funding was almost automatic for a well-written proposal. As a new tenure-track faculty member, Clare assumed the problem must have been her inability to write the proposal correctly and she made an appointment with the committee chair to seek his advice. When they met, he proceeded to tell her that the project was rejected because the committee felt it was not appropriate to do research on one's own students; completing the questionnaires or participating in the interviews would make the students vulnerable. He suggested that she use another population, a group of students completely removed from her program. Although eventually the project was approved, the experience left Clare shaken. If a small-scale project aimed at improving practice could not be approved in her local department without strong lobbying on her part, what chance would she have of obtaining large-scale funds for similar research?

Story #2. The University of Toronto has a fund to support the research efforts of new faculty. Given Clare's previous and ongoing work in preservice teacher education and the centrality of action research in the Mid-Town program, she asked for funding to do a large-scale project on the effects of student teachers and mentor teachers doing action research collaboratively during a practicum placement. The funding was approved in principle, but over a 14-month period her proposal was scrutinized by the university's ethical review committee and turned back six times (many other qualitative researchers were having similar problems with the review committee at the time). Each time the committee reviewed the submission, they requested further clarification, detail, and documentation. It became apparent that the main reason for requesting all this detail was that Clare was proposing to do research on her own students. Themes that emerged in the committee's letters were: students are placed in a dangerous position when they are part of a research study; students may feel pressured into becoming involved in a research project initiated by their professor; open-ended data gathering could be hazardous to students; and above all, there are legal risks involved in doing research on one's students. As she responded to each request for additional documentation, the intent of the study seemed to have been lost. Her goal, to increase her understanding of the process of student teachers and mentor teachers researching together and ultimately to enhance that process, seemed to be irrelevant to the committee. The tone of the correspondence suggested that the members of the committee conceptualized the relationship between professor and student as highly adversarial. But in fact Clare's problem usually was that too many students wanted to work with her; and they found collaboration between professor and student on research projects to be highly rewarding. She and her students transformed the relationship from professor and student to colleagues as the year progressed.

Apart from difficulties obtaining permission and funds to do the research, the other main challenge faced by preservice faculty who inquire into their own program is gaining respect and reward for their research. The research has at least three strikes against it: it is on teacher education, a low-status activity; it is practical in its setting and orientation; and it is study of one's own program rather than "objective" or "arm's length" inquiry. Accordingly, those who do research of this kind tend to have a lower status in their institution and not be rewarded as well as more "traditional" researchers in terms of tenure, promotion, salary increments, and so on. Once again, at OISE/UT we have been able to overcome these problems to a considerable extent, but the fact remains that teacher educators who do research on their own program have to fight continually for the recognition and reward more traditional researchers can take for granted. We have no regrets, for a range of reasons; but anyone contemplating self-study research in teacher education should be aware of this reality.

What can be done to ameliorate these two sets of difficulties? As discussed in the previous chapter, gaining greater support and respect for preservice education must be approached on two fronts, the ideological and the practical; and this applies to self-study research in particular. With regard to ideology, we think the main task is to show that researching one's own teaching is implied by the broad philosophy of teaching and teacher education that most SCDEs already officially endorse. We suggest making the case in terms such as the following.

General rationale for self-study research. Many contemporary writers are saying that a progressive or social constructivist approach to education—child-centered, inquiry-oriented, interactive, collaborative, communal, inclusive—is the only way for schools to go. Without such an approach, today's school students will not be engaged, will not learn, and will not become lifelong learners (Cohn & Kottkamp, 1993; Darling-Hammond, 1997; Meier, 1995; Wood, 1992, 1998). According to this approach, teachers do not just transmit content, they develop learning contexts or "environments" (Dewey, 1916). Accordingly, teachers must be researchers, observing in their classrooms, modifying the class routines and curriculum to meet the needs of their diverse students, and assessing the effects of these modifications. They have to get to know their students well and establish collaborative relationships with and among them. Activities must be initiated that engage the students rather than alienating them, and the class has to become a community to support these activities as well as meeting students' nonacademic needs.

In teacher education we have to model this approach to teaching, including the role of teacher-as-researcher. We cannot advocate an inquiry approach and then not practice it ourselves: the student teachers will not take us seriously and will not learn "how to do it." After their many years of "apprenticeship of observation" (Lortie, 1975, pp. 61–65) in the school and university system, talk is not enough; student teachers need strong modeling of a different approach, and firsthand experience of it. This is why action research done by student teachers is so crucial in a preservice program. And as we do research on our practice we must as far as possible involve our students, both to let them see the research process from within and to get their feedback. It is inconceivable that we could improve our practice significantly without constant input from the students experiencing the program.

On this view of teaching, teacher education, and teacher education research, then, it is disastrous for the field to put roadblocks in the way of self-study of preservice practice. Such research is an essential element in a whole approach to teaching and learning at many levels. And collaboration, community, and close interaction between professors, student teachers, and mentor teachers are essential to such research. Ways must be found to allow for and encourage all these features in teacher education, otherwise the whole enterprise will be jeopardized. Administering an SCDE with a preservice component is not just a technical task: one cannot simply apply a few rules about what counts as research and what is ethical and let the substance look after itself. Certain rules and procedures favor certain substantive goals. The current norms regarding research approval, support, and reward tend to steer preservice education away from the very kinds of educational practice we publicly espouse. We need to make explicit our philosophy of education and goals for preservice education, and in that context develop criteria, rules, and procedures with respect to research.

Beyond the SCDE itself, preservice researchers need support in other settings. In the larger university context, a strong SCDE voice should be heard supporting forms of research relevant to teacher education. A similar stance needs to be taken with the government and other external funding agencies. In the past, the attitude of SCDEs has often been that outside "experts," whether from the wider university or external bodies, know more than we do about research methods and we should largely accept their guidance. It has been assumed that there are certain general criteria of good research and these experts know best what they are. For example, until a few years ago, self-study research was automatically excluded at OISE/UT by the committee of experts used to adjudicate "transfer grant" funding from the Ministry of Education. But since, in fact, there is not just one type of good research, and many of the "experts" are biased toward types of research that can undermine good teaching and teacher education, faculties of education should engage in strong advocacy of different research paradigms rather than showing such deference.

Practical strategies for promoting self-study research. Such is the broad rationale, then, that we propose be promoted in SCDEs (and the larger university as much as possible) with a view to supporting research by preservice educators on their own program. At a more practical level, what can we do to make such research more feasible and respected? One step we have found useful at OISE/UT is to link up with other outstanding qualitative researchers in the school of education who are not currently in preservice education (such as Michael Connelly, Patrick Diamond, and others in the Center for Teacher Development). This gives us moral support, helps us refine our methodology, and indicates to the institution that a growing number of education academics are committed to this type of research.

Another strategy, discussed earlier, is to become involved in teaching courses on research methodology. This strengthens our presence and expertise in the area and helps increase the number of doctoral students in the institution who understand and respect qualitative and self-study approaches. In such courses we should to a significant extent discuss quantitative as well as qualitative methods, thus showing our interest in both. Initially, at least, we might invite experts on quantitative methods to do guest spots in our courses to help deal with more technical issues. Related to this, we should to some degree employ quantitative methods in our own research, even if it involves getting substantial assistance from research staff in the institution. This shows that we do not emphasize qualitative methods simply because we are prejudiced against quantitative methods or incapable of understanding them. Taking this point a step further, in teaching and writing on research methodology we should explore concepts such as validity, reliability, probability, replication, experimentation, sampling, and so on, showing their relevance to qualitative as well as quantitative research and thus indicating the similarity of logic between the two approaches.

At an even more practical level, it is important to ensure that faculty who understand and are sympathetic toward qualitative and self-study research are represented on the various approval committees. At the University of Toronto we now have a renowned expert in this area (Ardra Cole) on the central ethics review committee, and her presence has improved our situation greatly. Another very practical step is to submit our proposals to the more prestigious conferences and our manuscripts to the better-known refereed journals. This usually results in some initial rebuffs and a great deal of rewriting, but in the long run it helps increase respect for our research.

Finally, we would stress the need to make compromises as we try to gain acceptance for our type of research. Being strategic about the journals we publish in, the types of research contracts we pursue, and the place we give to quantitative research are examples of such compromise. We cannot afford simply to adopt a holier-than-thou attitude and wait for the world to catch up to us, since our ideas will hopefully continue to move ahead and we may always be out of step with accepted wisdom. Besides, there is much that we can learn from the ideas of other scholars, even when we disagree with their precise emphases. How far we can afford to go in making these compromises, however, will vary with our career and life circumstances, and these will change over time. Once again, we must not be too ambitious. The most important thing is to keep on researching our preservice program in whatever way we can, thereby discovering new ways to enhance our program and improve the learning experience of our students.

REFERENCES

Arends, R., & Winitzky, N. (1996). Program structures and learning to teach. In F. B. Murray (Ed.), *The teacher educator's handbook* (pp. 526–56). San Francisco: Jossey-Bass.

Barthes, R. (1970/1982). *Empire of signs*. Tr. R. Howard. New York: Hill & Wang.

Barthes, R. (1977). *Image, music, text*. Sel. & Tr. S. Heath. New York: Hill & Wang.

Beck, C. (1990). *Better schools: A values perspective*. London: Falmer.

Beck, C. (1993). *Learning to live the good life: Values in adulthood*. Toronto: OISE Press.

Beck, C., & Kosnik, C. (1998). A Canadian perspective on values education: The Ontario experience. *The Journal of Values Education, 2*, 32–43.

Beck, C., & Kosnik, C. (2001). From cohort to community in a preservice teacher education program. *Teaching and Teacher Education, 17*, 925–48.

Beck, C., Freese, A., & Kosnik, C. (2004). The preservice practicum: Learning through self-study in a professional setting. In J. Loughran, M-L. Hamilton, V. LaBoskey, & T. Russell (Eds.), *International handbook of self-study of teaching and teacher education practices* (pp. 1259–93). Dordrecht: Kluwer.

Benhabib, S. (1990). In the shadow of Aristotle and Hegel: Communicative ethics and current controversies in practical philosophy. In M. Kelly (Ed.), *Hermeneutics and critical theory in ethics and politics* (pp. 1–31). Cambridge, MA: MIT Press.

Berliner, D., & Biddle, B. (1995). *The manufactured crisis: Myths, fraud, and the attack on America's public schools*. Reading, MA: Addison-Wesley.

Berry, A., & Loughran, J. (2002). Developing an understanding of learning to teach in teacher education. In J. Loughran & T. Russell (Eds.), *Improving teacher education practices through self-study* (pp. 13–29). London: RoutledgeFalmer.

Borko, H., & Mayfield, V. (1995). The roles of cooperating teacher and university supervisor in learning to teach. *Teaching and Teacher Education, 11*(5), 501–18.

Bourdieu, P. (1977). *Outline of theory and practice*. Cambridge: Cambridge University Press.

Boyle-Baise, M. (2002). *Multicultural service learning: Educating teachers in diverse communities*. New York: Teachers College Press.

Britzman, D. (1991). *Practice makes practice: A critical study of learning to teach*. Albany, NY: State University of New York Press.

Brophy, J. (Ed.) (2002). *Social constructivist teaching: Affordances and constraints*. London: JAI/Elsevier Science.

Bullough, R., & Gitlin, A. (1995). *Becoming a student of teaching: Methodologies for exploring self and school context*. New York: Garland.

Carr, W. (1995). *For education: Towards critical educational inquiry*. Buckingham: Open University Press.

Carr, W., & Kemmis, S. (1986). *Becoming critical: Education, knowledge, and action research*. London: Falmer.

Casey, B., & Howson, P. (1993). Educating preservice students based on a problem-centered approach to teaching. *Journal of Teacher Education, 44*(5), 361–69.

Clandinin, J., Davies, A., Hogan, P., & Kennard, B. (Eds.) (1993). *Learning to teach, teaching to learn.* New York: Teachers College Press.

Cochran-Smith, M., & Lytle, S. (1993). *Inside/outside: Teacher research and knowledge.* New York: Teachers College Press.

Cochran-Smith, M., & Lytle, S. (2001). Beyond certainty: Taking an inquiry stance in practice. In A. Lieberman & L. Miller (Eds.), *Teachers caught in the action* (pp. 45–58). New York: Teachers College Press.

Cochran-Smith, M., Davis, D., & Fries, K. (2004). Multicultural teacher education: Research, practice, and policy. In J. Banks & C. McGee Banks (Eds.), *Handbook of research on multicultural education, 2nd edn.* (pp. 931–75). San Francisco: Jossey-Bass.

Cohn, M., & Kottkamp, R. (1993). *Teachers: The missing voice in education.* Albany, NY: State University of New York Press.

Cole, A., & Sorrill, P. (1992). Being an associate teacher: A feather in one's cap? *Education Canada,* Fall 1992, 40–48.

Dagenais, D., & Wideen, M. (1999). Teacher education at Simon Fraser University: Collaboration between professional cultures. In M. Wideen & P. Lemma (Eds.), *Ground level reform in teacher education: Changing schools of education* (pp. 169–83). Calgary: Detselig.

Darling-Hammond, L. (Ed.) (1994). *Professional development schools: Schools for developing a profession.* New York: Teachers College Press.

Darling-Hammond, L. (1997). *The right to learn.* San Francisco: Jossey-Bass.

Darling-Hammond, L. (1999). Educating teachers for the next century: Rethinking practice and policy. In G. Griffin (Ed.), *The education of teachers: 98th NSSE Yearbook, Part I* (pp. 221–56). Chicago: National Society for the Study of Education.

Darling-Hammond, L. (2002a). Learning to teach for social justice. In L. Darling-Hammond, J. French, & S. P. Garcia-Lopez, *Learning to teach for social justice* (pp. 1–7). New York: Teachers College Press.

Darling-Hammond, L. (2002b). Educating a profession for equitable practice. In L. Darling-Hammond, J. French, & S. P. Garcia-Lopez, *Learning to teach for social justice* (pp. 201–12). New York: Teachers College Press.

Darling-Hammond, L., & Macdonald, M. (2000). Where there is learning there is hope: The preparation of teachers at Bank Street College of Education. In L. Darling-Hammond (Ed.), *Studies of excellence in teacher education: Preparation at the graduate level* (pp. 1–95). Washington, DC: American Association of Colleges for Teacher Education.

Delpit, L. (1995). *Other people's children: Cultural conflict in the classroom.* New York: The New Press.

Derrida, J. (1967/1978). *Writing and difference.* Tr. A. Bass. London: Routledge and Kegan Paul.

Derrida, J. (1972/1982). *Margins of philosophy.* Tr. A. Bass. Chicago: University of Chicago Press.

Derrida, J. (1990). *Du droit à la philosophie.* Paris: Galilee.

Dewey, J. (1909/1975). *Moral principles in education.* Carbondale and Edwardsville: Southern Illinois University Press.

Dewey, J. (1916). *Democracy and education*. New York: Macmillan.

Dewey, J. (1929/1960). *The quest for certainty*. New York: Capricorn.

Dewey, J. (1934/1980). *Art as experience*. New York: Perigee.

Dewey, J. (1938). *Experience and education*. New York: Collier-Macmillan.

Ducharme, E., & Ducharme, M. (1999). Teacher educators and teachers: The need for excellence and spunk. In R. Roth (Ed.), *The role of the university in the preparation of teachers* (pp. 41–58). London: Falmer.

Elliott, J. (1991). *Action research for educational change*. Milton Keynes: Open University Press.

Elliott, J. (1997). School-based curriculum development and action research in the United Kingdom. In S. Hollingsworth (Ed.), *International action research* (pp. 17–28). London: Falmer.

Ewing, R., & Smith, D. (2002). Building communities in teacher education: The MTeach experience. In H. Christiansen & S. Ramadevi (Eds.), *Reeducating the educator: Global perspectives on community building* (pp. 151–68). Albany, NY: State University of New York Press.

Fosnot, C. (1989). *Enquiring teachers, enquiring learners: A constructivist approach for teaching*. New York: Teachers College Press.

Fosnot, C. (Ed.) (1996). *Constructivism: Theory, perspectives, and practice*. New York: Teachers College Press.

Foucault, M. (1997). *Michel Foucault: Ethics, subjectivity, and truth*. Ed. P. Rabinow. New York: The New Press.

Foucault, M. (1998). *Michel Foucault: Aesthetics, method, and epistemology*. Ed. J. D. Faubion. New York: The New Press.

Goodlad, J. (1990a). *Teachers for our nation's schools*. San Francisco: Jossey-Bass.

Goodlad, J. (1990b). Connecting the present to the past. In J. Goodlad, R. Soder, & K. Sirotnik (Eds.), *Places where teachers are taught* (pp. 3–39). San Francisco: Jossey-Bass.

Goodlad, J. (1994). *Educational renewal: Better teachers, better schools*. San Francisco: Jossey-Bass.

Goodwin, L. (1997). Historical and contemporary perspectives on multicultural teacher education: Past lessons, new directions. In J. King, E. Hollins, & W. Hayman (Eds.), *Preparing teachers for cultural diversity* (pp. 5–22). New York: Teachers College Press.

Goodwin, L. (2002). The case of one child: Making the shift from personal knowledge to professionally informed practice. *Teaching Education, 13*, 137–54.

Goodwin, A., & Lawrence, A. (2002). A professional development school for preparing teachers for urban schools. In G. Griffin & Associates, *Rethinking standards through teacher preparation partnerships* (pp. 69–87). Albany, NY: State University of New York Press.

Grossman, P., Valencia, S., Evans, K., Thompson, C., Martin, C., & Place, N. (2000). Transitions into teaching: Learning to teach writing in teacher education and beyond. *Journal of Literacy Research, 32*(4), 631–62.

Howey, K. (1996). Designing coherent and effective teacher education programs. In J. Sikula et al. (Eds.), *Handbook of research on teacher education, 2nd edn.* (pp. 143–70). New York: Macmillan.

Hubbard, R., & Power, B. (1993). *The art of classroom inquiry*. Portsmouth, NH: Heinemann.

Irvine, J. (2003). *Educating teachers for diversity: Seeing with a cultural eye.* New York: Teachers College Press.

Kagan, D. (1992). Professional growth among preservice and beginning teachers. *Review of Educational Research, 62*(2), 129–69.

Knowles, J. G., Cole, A., & Presswood, C. (1994). *Through preservice teachers' eyes: Exploring field experiences through narrative and inquiry.* New York: Merrill.

Kosnik, C., & Beck, C. (2000). The action research process as a means of helping student teachers understand and fulfill the complex role of the teacher. *Educational Action Research, 8*(1), 115–36.

Kosnik, C., & Beck, C. (2003). The contribution of faculty to community building in a teacher education program: A student teacher perspective. *Teacher Education Quarterly, 30*(3), 99–114.

Lemma, P. (1999). Developing leaders for learning communities: Faculty leadership for redesigning teacher education. In M. Wideen & P. Lemma (Eds.), *Ground level reform in teacher education: Changing schools of education* (pp. 185–214). Calgary: Detselig.

Liston, D., & Zeichner, K. (1991). *Teacher education and the social conditions of schooling.* New York: Routledge.

Lortie, D. (1975). *Schoolteacher: A sociological study.* Chicago: University of Chicago Press.

Lyotard, J.-F. (1984). *The postmodern condition.* Tr. G. Bennington & B. Massumi. Minneapolis: University of Minnesota Press.

Meier, D. (1995). *The power of their ideas.* Boston: Beacon.

Meier, D. (2000). *Will standards save public education?* Boston: Beacon.

Melnick, S., & Zeichner, K. (1997). Enhancing the capacity of teacher education institutions to address diversity issues. In J. King, E. Hollins, & W. Hayman (Eds.), *Preparing teachers for cultural diversity* (pp. 23–39). New York: Teachers College Press.

Miller, L., & Silvernail, D. (2000). Learning to become a teacher: The Wheelock way. In L. Darling-Hammond (Ed.), *Studies of excellence in teacher education: Preparation in the undergraduate years* (pp. 67–107). Washington, DC: American Association of Colleges for Teacher Education.

Noffke, S. (1997). Themes and tensions in US action research: Towards historical analysis. In S. Hollingsworth (Ed.), *International action research* (pp. 2–16). London: Falmer.

Nuthall, G. (2002). Social constructivist teaching and the shaping of students' knowledge and thinking. In J. Brophy (Ed.). *Social constructivist teaching: Affordances and constraints* (pp. 43–79). London: JAI/Elsevier Science.

Peterson, K. (1992). *Life in a crowded place: Making a learning community.* Porstmouth, NH: Heinemann.

Peterson, K., Benson, N., Driscoll, A., Narode, R., Sherman, D., & Tama, C. (1995). Preservice teacher education using flexible, thematic cohorts. *Teacher Education Quarterly, 22*(2), 29–42.

Phillips, D. (1995). The good, the bad, and the ugly: The many faces of constructivism. *Educational Researcher, 24*(7), 5–12.

Piaget, J. (1932). *The moral judgment of the child.* Tr. M. Gabain. London: Routledge & Kegan Paul.

Punch, K. (1998). *Introduction to social research: Quantitative and qualitative approaches.* London: Sage.

Richardson, V. (Ed.) (1997). *Constructivist teacher education: Building a world of new understandings.* London: Falmer.

Rorty, R. (1979). *Philosophy and the mirror of nature.* Princeton, NJ: Princeton University Press.

Rorty, R. (1985). Postmodernist bourgeois liberalism. In R. Hollinger (Ed.), *Hermeneutics and praxis* (pp. 214–21). Notre Dame, IN: University of Notre Dame Press.

Rorty, R. (1989). *Contingency, irony, & solidarity.* Cambridge, UK: Cambridge University Press.

Ross, D. (1987). Action research for preservice teachers: A description of why and how. *Peabody Journal of Education, 64*, 131–50.

Russell, T. (2002). Guiding new teachers' learning from classroom experience: Self-study of the faculty liaison role. In J. Loughran & T. Russell (Eds.), *Improving teacher education practices through self-study* (pp. 73–87). London: RoutledgeFalmer.

Samaras, A. (1998). Finding my way: Teaching methods courses from a sociocultural perspective. In A. Cole, R. Elijah, & G. Knowles (Eds.), *The heart of the matter: Teacher education and teacher education reform* (pp. 55–79). San Francisco: Caddo Gap Press.

Samaras, A. (2002). *Self-study for teacher educators: Crafting a pedagogy for educational change.* New York: Peter Lang.

Sarason, S. (1990). *The predictable failure of educational reform.* San Francisco: Jossey-Bass.

Schön, D. (1983). *The reflective practitioner: How professionals think in action.* New York: Basic Books.

Schön, D. (1987). *Educating the reflective practitioner.* San Francisco: Jossey-Bass.

Schoonmaker, F. (2002). *"Growing up" teaching: From personal knowledge to professional practice.* New York: Teachers College Press.

Slick, S. (1998). The university supervisor: A disenfranchised outsider. *Teaching and Teacher Education, 14*(8), 821–34.

Snyder, J. (2000). Knowing children—understanding teaching: The developmental teacher education program at the University of California-Berkeley. In L. Darling-Hammond (Ed.), *Studies of excellence in teacher education: Preparation at the graduate level* (pp. 97–172). Washington, DC: American Association of Colleges for Teacher Education.

Sosniak, L. A. (1999). Professional and subject matter knowledge for teacher education. In G. A. Griffin (Ed.), *The education of teachers: 98th NSSE Yearbook, Part I* (pp. 185–204). Chicago: National Society for the Study of Education.

Sternberg, R. (2003). What is an "expert student?" *Educational Researcher, 32*(8), 5–9.

Strauss, A., & Corbin, J. (1998). *Basics of qualitative research: Grounded theory procedures and techniques.* Newbury Park, CA: Sage.

Tom, A. (1997). *Redesigning teacher education.* Albany, NY: State University of New York Press

Vadeboncoeur, J. A. (1997). Child development and the purpose of education: A historical context for constructivism in teacher education. In V. Richardson (Ed.), *Constructivist teacher education: Building a world of new understandings* (pp. 15–37). London: Falmer.

Vavrus, M. (2002). *Transforming the multicultural education of teachers: Theory, research, and practice.* New York: Teachers College Press.

Villegas, A., & Lucas, T. (2002). *Educating culturally responsive teachers: A coherent approach.* Albany, NY: State University of New York Press.

Vygotsky, L. (1978). *Mind in society: The development of higher psychological processes.* Cambridge, MA: Harvard University Press.

Wasley, P. (1994). *Stirring the chalkdust: Tales of teachers changing classroom practice.* New York: Teachers College Press.

Wells, Gordon (1994). *Changing schools from within: Creating communities of inquiry.* Toronto/Portsmouth, NH: OISE Press/Heinemann.

Wideen, M., & Lemma, P. (Eds.). (1999). *Ground level reform in teacher education: Changing schools of education.* Calgary, Alberta: Detselig.

Wisniewski, R. (1990). Let's get on with it. *Phi Delta Kappan, 72,* 195–96.

Winitzky, N., Stoddart, T., & O'Keefe, P. (1992). Great expectations: Emergent professional development schools. *Journal of Teacher Education, 43*(1), 3–18.

Wood, G. (1992). *Schools that work.* New York: Penguin/Plume.

Wood, G. (1998). *A time to learn.* New York: Dutton.

Zeichner, K. (1990). Changing directions in the practicum: Looking ahead to the 1990s. *Journal of Education for Teaching, 16*(2), 105–32.

Zeichner, K. (1996). Designing educative practicum experiences for prospective teachers. In K. Zeichner, S. Melnick, & M. L. Gomez (Eds.), *Currents of reform in preservice teacher education* (pp. 215–34). New York: Teachers College Press.

Zeichner, K. (1998). The new scholarship in teacher education. Revised version (June 1998) of Division K vice presidential address presented at the annual meeting of AERA, San Diego, April, 1998. 46pp + refs.

ABOUT THE AUTHORS

Clive Beck is a Professor in the Department of Curriculum, Teaching and Learning at the Ontario Institute for Studies in Education, University of Toronto. In the Mid-Town preservice program he teaches social foundations and supervises practice teaching and action research. He is a past-president of the Philosophy of Education Society. His books include *Educational Philosophy and Theory*, *Better Schools*, and *Making a Difference in Teacher Education Through Self-Study*.

Clare Kosnik is an Associate Professor in the Department of Curriculum, Teaching and Learning at the Ontario Institute for Studies in Education, University of Toronto. She is currently on leave, serving as Director of the Teachers for a New Era research and development project at Stanford University. Her books include *Spelling in a Balanced Literacy Program*, *Primary Education: Goals, Processes and Practices*, and *Making a Difference in Teacher Education Through Self-Study*.

INDEX